E. I. du Pont, *Botaniste*
The Beginning of a Tradition

ELEUTHÈRE IRÉNÉE DU PONT

E. I. du Pont, *Botaniste*

The Beginning of a Tradition

NORMAN B. WILKINSON

Published for the
Eleutherian Mills-Hagley Foundation

The University Press of Virginia
Charlottesville

THE UNIVERSITY PRESS OF VIRGINIA
Copyright © 1972 by the
Eleutherian Mills-Hagley Foundation

First published 1972

ISBN: cloth, 0–8139–0399–8; paper, 0–8139–0398–X
Library of Congress Catalog Card Number: 76–171485
Printed in the United States of America

Frontispiece: Eleuthère Irénée du Pont at about twenty-five years of age, by an unknown artist.

Endpapers: Illustrations from F. A. Michaux's *Histoire des arbres forestiers de l'Amérique septentrionale* for which E. I. du Pont provided seed and nut specimens.

Decorative devices: Floral motifs sketched by the daughters of E. I. du Pont to be used as needlework patterns.

Contents

Illustrations		vi
Preface		ix
Introduction		1
Chapter I	The Ground Is Prepared	5
Chapter II	The Transplantation	15
Chapter III	The Gardens of the Republic	27
Chapter IV	The New Home	49
Chapter V	Botanizing in Brandywine Woods	61
Chapter VI	The Gardens at Eleutherian Mills	67
Chapter VII	Gardeners of the Second Generation	80
Chapter VIII	Winterthur	99
Chapter IX	Longwood Gardens	107
Chapter X	The New and Old Gardens at Eleutherian Mills	120
Appendix	Eleutherian Mills: Garden and Orchard List	133

Illustrations

Eleuthère Irénée du Pont   *Frontispiece*

Figures

1. Sophie Madeleine du Pont   xii
2. Detail of E. I. du Pont's passport   3
3. Bois-des-Fossés   6
4. René Desfontaines   12
5. Conservatory in the Jardin des Plantes   13
6. Pages from E. I. du Pont's botanical notebook   16–17
7. E. I. du Pont's passport   19
8. Seeds sent to France by E. I. du Pont, 1802   24
9. E. I. du Pont's packing list of seeds, 1802   25
10. Michaux's map of the Bergen's Wood–Hackensack area   28
11. Michaux's sketch of the French government garden in New Jersey   30
12. *Pinckneya pubens*   33
13. E. I. du Pont's letter to Mme. Bonaparte   34–35
14. Conservatory at Malmaison   37
15. Orchard plan for Eleutherian Mills   50–51
16. Front view of the residence at Eleutherian Mills, 1823   54
17. Sketch of Eleutherian Mills, 1817   55
18. François André Michaux   60
19. Packing list of plant materials E. I. du Pont sent Michaux   63
20. Barn at Eleutherian Mills   68
21. The du Pont garden, 1873   70
22. Design of the du Pont garden, about 1880   72

23. Pages from Victorine du Pont's botany manual   82–83

24. Herbarium specimen picked by Sophie du Pont   84

25. Wedding trees at Louviers   86

26. Map of du Pont homes on the Brandywine   88

27. Winterthur, 1884   100

28. Residence and garden, Winterthur, 1900   103

29. Peirce's Park, 1884   108

30. Avenue of trees in Longwood Gardens, 1910   109

31. The first garden at Longwood, 1909   116

32. Classical gardens at Eleutherian Mills   121

33. Terraced gardens at the Crowninshield home   126

34. Conifers in the Crowninshield gardens   127

35. Archaeological excavation at Eleutherian Mills   130

Plates

1. Amphitheater in the Jardin des Plantes   21

2. Dwarf and espaliered fruit trees at Bois-des-Fossés today   22

3. Malmaison   39

4. Vauréal   40

5. View from the rear piazza of Eleutherian Mills   57

6. Brandywine Woods   58

7. Blossom of hybrid horsechestnut tree   75

8. Watercolor of lily by Sophie du Pont   76

9. Upper Louviers   93

10. Entrance to Upper Louviers garden   94

11. Azalea woods at Winterthur   111

12. Daffodils along banks of Clenny Run, Winterthur   112

13. Fall display in the conservatory, Longwood Gardens   113

14. Fountains at Longwood Gardens   114

15. Eleutherian Mills   123

16. Raceway in Hagley Yard   124

Who loves a garden still his Eden keeps,
Perennial pleasures plants, and wholesome harvests reaps.
                                        Amos Bronson Alcott

Preface

THIS book came to be written in search of an answer to a simple but puzzling question: why did Eleuthère Irénée du Pont, a man who had earned his living as a powderman and then as a printer and publisher, state his occupation as "Botaniste" on his passport when he left France for America in 1799?

The explanation offered in this account, standing alone, is only a fragment of personal biography, an interesting facet of a man's life of seemingly limited interest. But the search for the answer has led to sources that place it within the much broader context of botany and horticulture in France and the United States at the beginning of the nineteenth century.

Du Pont family and business papers numbering millions of items that range over a century and a half, from the 1750s to the early 1900s, are housed in the Eleutherian Mills Historical Library near Greenville, Delaware. They were created by five generations of the family in France and the United States and are organized into two major collections, the Winterthur Manuscripts and the Longwood Manuscripts. The correspondence, memoranda, notes, plant lists, sketches, and accounts in these two groups have been the principal sources used by the writer. Quoted materials originally in French have been translated except in one or two instances where the "flavor" or unique quality of the passage would be lost in translation.

The papers of Pierre S. du Pont (1870–1954), also in the Eleutherian Mills Historical Library, were useful in telling the earlier history of Longwood Gardens; and its library, administrative files, and several of its retired employees furnished information on more recent developments. The strictly factual was garnished with family anecdotes told to the author by W. W. Laird.

The Archives Nationales in Paris furnished supplemental information about the gardens maintained by the French government in the United States, and about the work of André and François André Michaux in promoting horticultural interchange between the two countries. Descriptive details of the French government garden at Hackensack, New Jersey, were obtained from an article, "André Michaux's New Jersey Garden and Pierre Paul Saulnier, Journeyman Gardener," by William J. Robbins and Mary C. Howson, published in the *Proceedings of the American Philosophical Society,* Volume 102, Number 4, August 1958. F. A. Michaux's book on American silviculture, *Histoire des arbres forestiers de l'Amérique septentrionale* (Paris, 1810–1813), and its English language edition, *The North American Sylva* (Philadelphia, 1817–1819), were scanned with profit. An appreciative summation of the work of the two Michauxs by Gilbert Chinard is found in *Les botanistes français en Amérique du nord avant 1850* (Paris, 1957).

Glimpses of Josephine Bonaparte at Malmaison as patroness of botanists and gardeners were found in *Le jardin de la Malmaison,* by E. P. Ventenat (Paris, 1804); in *Les roses de l'impératrice Josephine,* by J. Gravereaux (Paris, 1912); and in E. P. Knapton's *Empress Josephine* (Cambridge, Mass., 1963).

E. M. Fleming and C. Gordon Tyrell have each contributed articles on the history of the Winterthur property and the development of its gardens to the *Winterthur Portfolio I* (Wilmington, Delaware, 1964). More recently has appeared *The Gardens of Winterthur in All Seasons,* by Harold Bruce (New York, 1968), illustrated by the photographic artistry of Gottlieb and Hilda Hampfler.

I would like to thank Dr. Russell J. Seibert, director, and Dr. Donald G. Huttleston, taxonomist, of Longwood Gardens for their appraisals of the manuscript. Dr. George H. Lawrence, director of the Hunt Botanical Library, Pittsburgh, and Dr. Walter M. Whitehill, director of the Library of the Boston Athenaeum, also generously gave time to read the text and offer suggestions.

From the inception of this study Dr. Walter J. Heacock, director of the Eleutherian Mills-Hagley Foundation, and David T. Gilchrist, director of publications, have given helpful counsel, and I have had assistance researching it from Mrs. Gordon K. Pizor and Mrs. Curtis M. Hinsley of the Foundation staff. Mrs. Curtis B. Cameron prepared the manuscript, and Frank T. Herzog and Charles A. Foote, Foundation photographers, Gottlieb Hampfler, photographer at Longwood Gardens, and Robert C. Lautman have contributed illustrations in both original and copy form. The map showing the locations of the du Pont homes was adapted and drawn by Wilford L. Fletcher, Jr., a Foundation staff artist, from an 1826 property survey.

I am particularly indebted for guidance among the extensive du Pont family papers in the Eleutherian Mills Historical Library to Dr. John B. Riggs, Mrs. George Windell, and Mrs. David N. Low. Their collaboration expedited research and led to the discovery of a number of illustrations reproduced in this book. Unless otherwise credited, all illustrations come from the collections of the Eleutherian Mills-Hagley Foundation.

Books, like gardens, are seldom the creation of one individual. Both substance and form of this book are due in large measure to the enthusiasm and assistance of friends and professional colleagues.

Greenville, Delaware
May 1972

Fig. 1 A miniature of Sophie Madeleine du Pont painted by
Joseph Bouton about the time of her marriage in 1791.
Courtesy of Estate of William du Pont, Jr.

Introduction

Apart from the interest I have always found in botany,
the thought that I can share it with you makes it
infinitely more delightful to me.
> E. I. du Pont to his wife Sophie, 1799

I T WAS springtime in Paris.

On a morning early in May 1799, a tall man in his late twenties strode quickly through the quiet streets of the awakening city on his way to the Jardin des Plantes, the botanical gardens that lay to the east of the Cathedral of Notre Dame and opposite the Quai de la Rapée on the river Seine.

At the Jardin des Plantes (plate 1) an early morning course in botany was being offered on alternate days by Professor Citizen René Desfontaines, and the man hurrying to class did not want to be late. He was a regular attender at the popular classes of M. Desfontaines, rising at 5 A.M. to get to a 6 A.M. class. He paid close attention, took scrupulous notes during the three-hour session of lectures and demonstrations, and then by 9:30 A.M. had returned to his job at the firm of Imprimerie de Du Pont on the rue de l'Oratoire, where he assisted his father, Pierre Samuel du Pont de Nemours, in managing a publishing and printing business. As soon as he had opportunity he transcribed his rough notes into neater, more legible, and fuller form for a very practical reason, and for a sentimental one.

To his young wife, Sophie, living with their three children on the family farm at Chevannes, near Nemours, some sixty miles from Paris, Eleuthère Irénée du Pont declared in one of his frequent letters that he took careful notes "so that they may be useful for my Sophie and her little ones. Apart from the interest I have always found in botany, the thought that I can share it with you makes it infinitely more delightful to me." And then, fondly, he added, "How much more pleasure I would have, my Sophie, if you could study with me. How we would enjoy these walks at six o'clock in the morning in

1

the groves of the Jardin des Plantes!" A pleasing, romantic suggestion, but hardly practicable for a mother caring for three small children sixty miles away.

Had Sophie and the children been living in Paris, there is little doubt that she would have made every effort to accompany her husband, for in her reply she told him, "I am really sorry that I cannot share your study of botany; you know how I love it and the pleasure of studying with you would be doubled by my interest." Irénée's affectionate response assured Sophie that he had no amusements except the time spent at the Jardin des Plantes, "where the pleasure is greater because it concerns you; it seems as if I had consecrated those three hours to you and that you are pleased."

Du Pont was diligently studying botany before breakfast for reasons other than his liking for the subject and wishing to share its pleasures with his wife and children. He was making serious preparations for a momentous event that he, his father, and his elder brother Victor had been plannning for over a year. They and their families were getting ready to leave France; they were migrating to the United States where they were going to "transplant" themselves and settle somewhere on the American frontier, then the western, backwoods regions of Virginia and Kentucky.

In this new home, which Irénée spoke of as "the bright new side of the cheese," they had dreams of building a "Rural Society," a carefully planned colony in the wilderness where survival might depend upon living off and developing the resources of the land about them. Irénée, with his knowledge of plants, shrubs, trees, crops, and the medicinal uses of herbs, and his skill in growing things, would be important to the success of this colonizing venture. It was for this reason the younger son paid close attention to the lectures of M. Desfontaines, carefully reviewed his notes, and, when time permitted, read books and articles on botany and horticulture. Thus, when the moment came to fill out his passport in June 1799, he did not declare either of his earlier occupations, first powder maker, then printer, but wrote on the prescribed line what he believed his future vocation would be: "Botaniste" (fig. 2).

One wonders at the presumption of young du Pont in declaring himself a botanist after attending only eight lectures on the subject. His care in taking voluminous notes on de Jussieu's system of botanical classification—into classes, orders, genera, species—and on

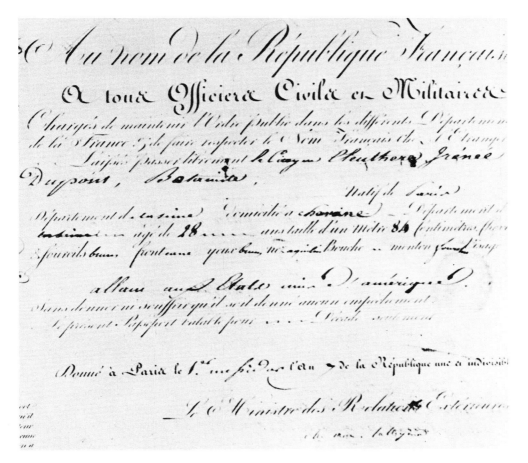

Fig. 2 Detail of passport issued to Eleuthère Irénée du Pont, *Botaniste*, in 1799. Courtesy of Delaware State Archives.

the physiology and nomenclature of plants indicates he was eager to learn a great deal in a brief time, but this was only elementary and introductory, far from qualifying him as a professionally trained botanist.

It would have been far more valid to have given his occupation as printer and publisher on his passport, for this had been the family business in which he had been assisting his father for the past eight years. Editing the text and reading the proofs of the Duc de La

Rochefoucauld-Liancourt's multivolume *Voyage dans les Etats-Unis, 1795–1797*, the firm's last publication, consumed all his working hours after returning from classes at the Jardin des Plantes during the spring weeks of 1799. Another occupation he could have stated validly was powder maker. As a youth of sixteen he had been employed by the Régie des Poudres, the government's powder-making bureau, first at the Arsenal in Paris that Antoine Lavoisier had directed and then in the powder mills at Essonne, which he had left in 1791. Why, then, did du Pont profess to be a botanist to the emigration authorities who would allow or deny him passage to America?

The answer may be that at the tag end of a decade of revolutionary violence marked by coups and government upheavals, imprisonments and surveillances, guillotining and exiling, conscripting and campaigning, a botanist was considered far less essential to France's war effort than either a powder maker or a printer. It is questionable, however, that du Pont resorted to a subterfuge of this kind to get out of the country. When he wrote "Botaniste" on his passport, he was declaring what he thought was going to be his future occupation in his new home in the United States. This was a change of career; he was leaving powder making and printing behind him.

As one of the managers of the projected Rural Society, to be named "Pontiania," his responsibilities in establishing the new colony on the American frontier would include developing the land, supervising farming operations, planting orchards, creating gardens, and learning to make the best use of the trees, plants, and herbs indigenous to the locality. The prospectus that his father had prepared to advertise this colonizing venture stated that Irénée du Pont "had had much experience of business methods in France, in agriculture, manufactures and the useful arts." For many reasons his father, who had been a public figure active in government and political affairs since the 1760s, was far more suspect of being denied permission to leave France. But he was departing as a "savant voyageur," an explorer-scientist, under the aegis of the Institut National, the country's leading learned society, of which he was a member, commissioned by it as a naturalist to explore the United States, to study and write of its flora and fauna, and to send specimens of these back to France. Irénée, freshly schooled in the botanical lectures of M. Desfontaines, was to serve as his assistant and secretary in this assignment.

CHAPTER I

The Ground Is Prepared

His tastes are simple: botany, hunting, fishing, rural responsibilities. In sum, all the joys one can find in country living and in a happy household are his.

Mrs. Victor du Pont, of E. I. du Pont, 1800

IRÉNÉE du Pont's love of botany was not a new interest freshly aroused by the engrossing lectures of M. Desfontaines at the Jardin des Plantes in Paris. From the age of three his boyhood had been spent amid growing things on the family's farm-estate, Bois-des-Fossés—"the wood of the moats"—near the village of Chevannes, near Nemours, in the Gâtinais, south of Paris (fig. 3). His father had acquired the property of over four hundred acres in 1774, and it remained the family home for the next twenty-five years. The enforced time spent away from this lovely place in the country was endured rather than enjoyed.

The farm stood close by woods and fields and stretches of meadowland. From the orchard came apples, peaches, pears, and cherries and other fruits in season. Walnuts and chestnuts were part of the harvest. Arbors and trellises supported the grapes grown for the September vintage, and close to the house were herb, vegetable, and flower gardens. Espaliered trees covered the terraced garden walls, and clumps of honeysuckle gave off their elusive fragrance in the damp of early morning (plate 2). There were cows to be milked, poultry to be tended, and sheep to be clipped in shearing season. Pets—dogs, rabbits, doves, and canaries—were there to play with and while away the time. Growing up in this setting implanted a love for the rural life in du Pont and stimulated a vast curiosity about the things of nature that surrounded him. Years later, after they had settled in America in 1800, first at Bon Séjour in Bergen Point, New Jersey, and then at Eleutherian Mills on Brandywine Creek near Wilmington, Delaware, the family clung to this familiar and satis-

5

Fig. 3 Bois-des-Fossés, the du Pont home in France. Courtesy of Winterthur Museum.

fying rural farm-and-garden way of life, developing at their Delaware home many of the things they had grown up with at Bois-des-Fossés.

Pierre Samuel du Pont de Nemours, at one time administrator general of agriculture and commerce in the French government, and a writer on agricultural and horticultural subjects, guided his son into the joyful discoveries of natural history. One of the earliest lessons Irénée learned was contained in a mildly reproving note written by his father from Paris when the boy was eleven years old:

I want to write you on a very *lofty* subject—birds' nests. . . . A nest is a little home which is used by a father and mother for the care of their children. Eggs are children in swaddling clothes and are so dear to their parents that they will go without food or water and even risk their lives rather than cease to care for them and keep them warm. They are therefore capable of much tenderness and love. They are made differently from us but have the same affections that we do.

6

I know very well that if a great animal as much stronger than I am as you are stronger than a little bird came to steal Victor and Irénée, or only one of them, your Mother and I would be in agony, and if I could not kill him to defend you I think I should die of grief. That thought makes me very unwilling to cause a sorrow that would be so great to me to any of these little animals with which we are not at war. Think it over!

Since education is useful I allowed you to take the first nests because I thought it gave you a lesson in natural history; but now that you have learned it and know the different kinds, why go on? Useless cruelty cannot attract my children.

Among family papers there is a lengthy memorandum, a copy of Rousseau's "Lettres elémentaires sur la botanique à Mme. de Luxembourg," which appears to have been an exercise assigned to Irénée by his father or by a tutor he had when he was fifteen. The tutor was Joseph Franz Jacquin, five years his senior, who had been engaged to tutor Irénée in Latin and chemistry. There is strong likelihood that botany and natural history were part of the curriculum, for in 1791 Jacquin joined the faculty of the University of Vienna as assistant professor of botany and chemistry, and in 1823 he became director of the botanical garden in Vienna.

Du Pont de Nemours was a Physiocrat, a prolific writer who expounded the principles of those who believed in the "Rule of Nature"—that the well-being of man stemmed from the soil; earth, air, and water were the vital elements from which he derived all sustenance and happiness. The essence of this philosophy he epitomized by going back to a quotation from Cicero, "Nihil est agricultura melius, nihil uberius, nihil dulcius, nihil homine libero dignius," which translated reads, "Nothing excels the cultivation of the earth, nothing is more universal, nothing more enjoyable, nothing more befitting a free man." In more florid style he romanticized this sentiment when he wrote, "The lovers of Flora find it hard to leave her laughing valleys and delicious woodlands." It is interesting to note that when he married a second time, in 1795, du Pont de Nemours married the widow of Pierre Poivre, formerly a governor of Isle de France and Isle de Bourbon but possibly better known as an eminent naturalist.

Not long after his arrival in this country in 1800, the elder du Pont was asked by his friend Thomas Jefferson to offer suggestions for a plan of education to be used in American schools. In a memorandum submitted to Jefferson he recommended the teaching of natural history, some instruction in animals and common plants, "interesting at all ages," and particularly botany, a useful science that afforded recreation, besides being entertaining, healthful, and a relief from the routine activities of the day.

When his duties as a government official kept him in Paris for prolonged periods, Pierre Samuel's letters to his son Irénée frequently contained instructions about planting the new trees he was having sent to Bois-des-Fossés; when the grapevines should be dressed and the fruit trees pruned; where to send for rose bushes; and often his letters contained packets of seeds such as tarragon, wild chicory, leek, and garden cress. Irénée was then too young to do the heavier farm and garden chores but he watched and helped Coeur du Roi, the farm manager, and the gardeners Langrevin and Drouet.

On Irénée's fifteenth birthday his brother Victor wrote him from Lyons apologizing for not having had time to make up a "natural history box" to send as a gift; in its place he sent a bouquet of flowers, but he promised to bring the box when he left Lyons for home. On another occasion, after he had been away many months, Victor wrote to chide Irénée for being a poor correspondent—he wrote only because he wanted Victor to send him certain kinds of seeds that could be obtained nowhere else but in the vicinity of Marseilles, where Victor happened to be. Good-naturedly the elder brother informed him, "Your seeds will be sent. . . . I found them hard to get for I went to at least twelve gardeners without finding them."

At the age of sixteen Irénée left Bois-des-Fossés to live in Paris, where he went to work in the Arsenal. For the next twelve years the country place became a second home to which he and Victor and their father returned whenever time allowed. To escape the confinement of the city at other times he explored the countryside around Paris, on some trips probably accompanied by his father. One of his excursions took him to the Montmorency Valley in July 1788, specifically to collect botanical specimens; undoubtedly trips were made elsewhere for the same purpose.

After several years of routine clerical and bookkeeping chores and a year's experience at the Essonne powder mills, Irénée grew restive and began thinking about changing his occupation. In 1791 he confided to Victor that he would like to sign on as a naturalist with the French navy, which was preparing a scientific expedition to make a round-the-world cruise to gather and bring home natural history specimens. Victor, now in the French consular service and stationed in Philadelphia, thought he was very foolish:

You write of being employed as a naturalist and I think that absolute folly. The studies and examinations you have had would surely make it possible for you to fill a position as engineer or some other military employment. If, as seems possible, our government becomes absolutely republican, the sciences will be neglected and ten years from now a poor naturalist will die of starvation.

Victor's disheartening but mistaken advice may have changed Irénée's mind; he gave up the idea of becoming a naturalist and joined his father in the printing business. Soon afterwards he married Sophie Madeleine Dalmas and took his bride to Bois-des-Fossés to become mistress of the household. Mme. du Pont, his mother, had died in 1784.

Sophie, in her seventeenth year, was very young to assume the task of managing the country home, but several servants helped her, and the heavy gardening and farming chores were done by hired men. Separated much of the time from her husband at work in Paris, she relied upon the advice and instructions his letters contained about planting, pruning, harvesting, and selling the surplus farm products. Periodic scarcities of food in Paris prompted her to send some of the foodstuffs to Irénée and "Bon Papa," and they were to sell what they did not need. Typical was one shipment sent by coach consisting of four pâtés, the main ingredient of which was hare, and thirty pounds of butter. In 1793, her father-in-law, harassed by political persecution, came home to Bois-des-Fossés, where he stayed for a time and helped Sophie manage the farm. A new member of the family, Victorine, Sophie and Irénée's first child, had recently been born. The mother's letters to her husband contained much family and neighborhood news, but she too was alive to the richness and beauty of the gardens and woods where she spent many pleasant hours with the baby in the warm sunshine.

A typical letter was this one written in early spring 1793, when leaves were beginning to green and buds to form: "Yesterday was clear and we spent most of the day in the garden. Our dear father worked at his peach trees and we watched him." A freshly plucked flower was often inserted in her letters, usually the first flower of the season—"I found this little hawthorn flower; it is the first in our field, and as the first flowers and fruits are always for the one we love best, I send it to you." A little while later another letter held the first columbine that Sophie and the baby had found on one of their walks. To Irénée in his Paris apartment these tokens were a delight, but they made him homesick and more determined to join his family as soon as he could get out of the strife-torn city.

On pleasant evenings in early summer, supper was eaten in the garden, with the first strawberries of the season for dessert. But Irénée's absence clouded Sophie's enjoyment: "There are quantities of roses and honeysuckle but flowers are not beautiful to me except when you are with your sweetheart." When Sophie discovered a new flower unknown to her, she enclosed it in her letter and asked Irénée to identify it, for "no one here knows what it is; I will keep one like it for your botanical collection." The young mother asked her husband to bring some pins on his next trip home; she was making a collection of butterflies for him which she was sure he would like.

On Sophie's birthday, her father-in-law, a gallant gentleman who tried his hand at nearly everything, including verse, wrote these lines in botanical idiom to celebrate the occasion:

> De mes vieux ans vous charmez le destin
> Dernière Rose de ma vie!
> Vous aurez, ma fille chérie,
> Les dernières de mon jardin.

Little Victorine, in the early walking and exploring stage, looked forward to her father's visits, for he spent much time with her, teaching her the names of the animals and plants they discovered on their rambles. And when the stage took him back to Paris, she could not believe he had gone away; he was out hunting or in the garden and would soon come back. Impatiently she awaited his return, eager to show him all the new flowers she had discovered during his absence.

Regularly, in planting season, Irénée sent from Paris a supply of new young trees to replace those which had died at Bois-des-Fossés. Sophie had planted those for which Irénée had designated the locations, but the others were heeled in until his next visit, when together they would choose the best places. She enumerated for her husband the tasks she had in mind for the hired man: cut down the hedge around the nursery, trim the hedge along the field, cut back the thorn hedge, trim the poplars, plow the garden, and dig holes for the new trees. And Sophie made it a practice to let him know what success they were having, information he was always pleased to receive: "All that we sowed or planted is growing. Most of the trees have their leaves out; so have all the lilacs, the laburnums, some thorns and many fruit trees." When the peaches were picked in September, a basketful of the finest was sent to Irénée in the city, which he acknowledged by saying, "They were as fresh as if they had just been gathered." In the vintage season Sophie's days were long and strenuous, as she informed her husband, "I have been up since six o'clock and it has been hard to find a moment to write this line. We have thirty-one vintagers, so I have plenty to do."

A visit to her own family, the Dalmases, in the spring of 1796, brought Sophie and little Victorine to Paris, and it was necessary for Irénée to go to Bois-des-Fossés to superintend the planting. Sophie was appalled at the unrest and turbulence in the city. She longed for a quick return to the quiet security of her country home, to be with her husband and "to see the new flowers and the sweet renewal of all nature." Irénée responded, telling her about the trees and vines being pruned, the planting of the corn, peas, and potatoes, and the sudden change from winter to summer. "Everything is green, everything is growing, pushing through the ground with wonderful rapidity. The birds, the nightingales mingle their delicious songs day and night. . . . I kiss the bouquet I am sending you."

During the remaining three years before they sailed for America in October 1799, in which time two more children, Evelina and Alfred Victor, were born, Bois-des-Fossés continued to be home for the family. The decision to leave *la belle patrie* for the Promised Land of America was made in family council sometime in 1797, but preparations for the pending departure did not cause them to neglect the property. The gardens were kept up, new flowers and shrubs were introduced, dead or unsightly fruit and ornamental trees were replaced with fresh stock, and acorns and chestnuts were planted. Habitually Sophie or one of the children carefully picked the first flower of each type as it appeared and enclosed it in her letter to Irénée in Paris. When the time came for departure, sadly and with heavy hearts they left this cherished homestead, leasing it to Philippe Harmand, a cousin of Irénée's.

Fig. 4 René Desfontaines, professor of botany, Ecole de Botanique, Jardin des Plantes. Courtesy of Muséum National d'Histoire Naturelle.

For more than twenty years Bois-des-Fossés had been a "nursery" for Irénée du Pont. He had learned much about botany by observing and collecting and by being gardener and grafter. He had gained a wealth of practical knowledge about growing things by being farmer and orchardist. But he had never had any formal academic instruction in botany until the early months of 1799, when we first met him, shortly after dawn, hurrying through the streets of Paris on his way to M. Desfontaines's lectures at the Jardin des Plantes. Of this excellent teacher it was said that "his course was followed with unequalled enthusiasm." And, of the status of botany as a science at the end of the eighteenth century, "In botany France had regained first place."

As the center for botanical study, the Paris gardens that had been established in 1635 narrowly escaped destruction in 1793. Their earlier names, Jardins Royaux, or Jardin du Roi, associated them with the royal family, and those revolutionists who wished to erase every last trace of the deposed Bourbon monarchy came very close to destroying them. Fortunately the influential M. Joseph Lakanal,

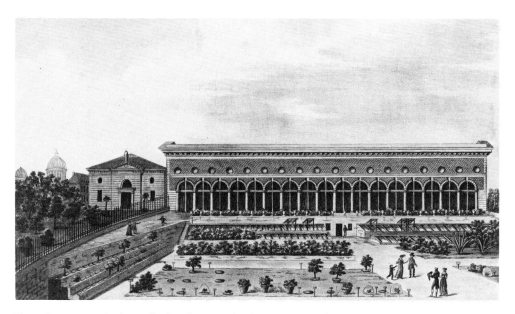

Fig. 5 Conservatory in the Jardin des Plantes, early 1800s. Courtesy of Hunt Botanical Library.

president of the Committee for Public Instruction, opposed this senseless vandalism. Aided by André Thouin, director of the gardens, by L. J. Daubenton, an eminent naturalist, and by Desfontaines, he prevailed upon the new government to save them. To satisfy republican sensibilities, the institution was reorganized and the name changed to Muséum National d'Histoire Naturelle, or the National Museum of Natural History, and the botanical division of the museum soon acquired the more popular name of Jardin des Plantes, the Botanical Garden. Under Thouin's management the gardens were expanded and improved, new buildings erected, graduates of the Ecole de Botanique were encouraged to go to French colonies to collect specimens and establish gardens, and from many parts of the world new flowers, plants, and trees were sent back to enrich the Jardin des Plantes. In Chapter III we shall learn of the contributions made to his "alma mater" by Irénée du Pont, amateur botanist, in his new home in America.

CHAPTER II

The Transplantation

Botany, which I began to study in your school, has been a great pleasure to me in this country where its forms are so new to me.

E. I. du Pont to André Thouin

THE summer months of 1799 were busy ones for the du Pont family. The father's chief concern was to find investors for the company he was organizing, Du Pont (de Nemours) Père, Fils et Compagnie, which would launch the frontier colony in America. Victor made the arrangements for the family's passage across the Atlantic on a vessel named the *American Eagle,* and Irénée handled the sale of the presses, type, paper stock, and books and arranged the leasing of Bois-des-Fossés to the new occupants. Well in advance of the sailing date, an agreement was made with a nurseryman named de Luines to send to the du Ponts in the United States any types of trees and plants that they might request after they had settled in their new home.

Another venture born in the fertile mind of du Pont de Nemours was the purchase and landscaping of a number of lots in the new Federal city rising on the banks of the Potomac River. Well informed on American events, he knew the seat of government would soon be moving from Philadelphia to Washington. Public buildings were going up and foreign nations would be establishing embassies. Congressmen, senators, and government officials would need homes; hence there would be a demand for building sites attractively planted and landscaped. In his father's judgment, Irénée, the botanist of the family, could undertake this assignment. The powderman-printer turned botanist no doubt felt more confident of his ability as a landscape architect knowing that stowed away in his baggage was a green binder bearing the title "Botanique: Méthode du Jardin des Plantes," which held over two hundred pages of tightly written, neatly arranged notes, the substance of M. Desfontaines's lectures (fig. 6).

After a long, harrowing, and nearly disastrous crossing, the family

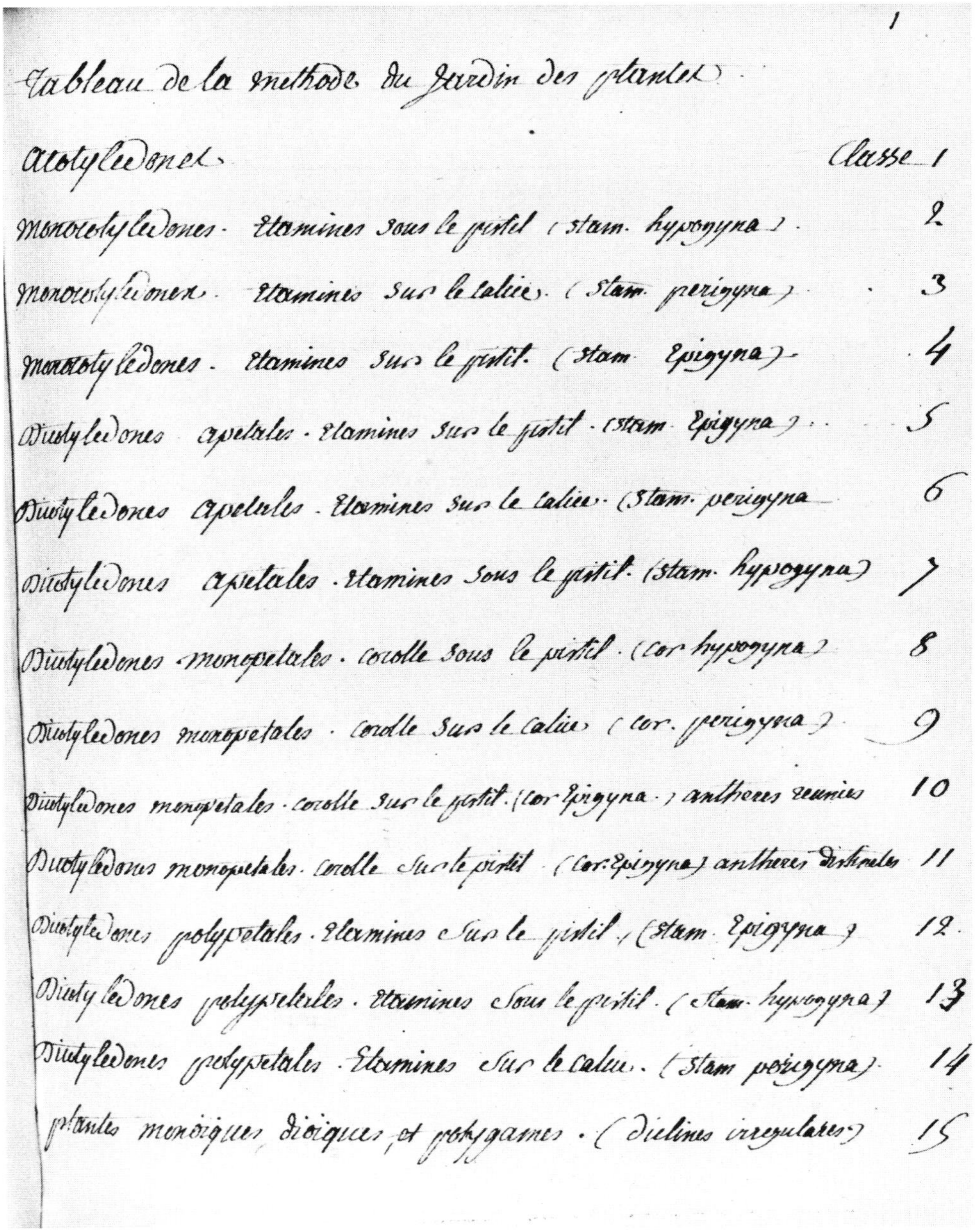

1

Tableau de la methode du Jardin des plantes

Acotyledones.   Classe 1

Monocotyledones. Etamines sous le pistil (stam. hypogyna).   2

Monocotyledones. Etamines sur le calice (stam. perigyna)   · 3

Monocotyledones. Etamines sur le pistil. (stam. Epigyna)   · 4

Dicotyledones apetales. Etamines sur le pistil. (stam Epigyna) ·   5

Dicotyledones apetales. Etamines sur le calice. (stam. perigyna   6

Dicotyledones apetales. Etamines sous le pistil. (stam. hypogyna)   7

Dicotyledones monopetales. corolle sous le pistil. (cor hypogyna)   8

Dicotyledones monopetales. corolle sur le calice (cor. perigyna)   9

Dicotyledones monopetales. corolle sur le pistil. (cor Epigyna) antheres reunies   10

Dicotyledones monopetales. corolle sur le pistil (cor. Epigyna) antheres distinctes   11

Dicotyledones polypetales. Etamines sur le pistil. (stam Epigyna)   12

Dicotyledones polypetales. Etamines sous le pistil. (stam hypogyna)   13

Dicotyledones polypetales. Etamines sur le calice. (stam perigyna)   14

plantes monoïques, dioïques, et polygames. (dielines irregulares)   15

Fig. 6 Pages from E. I. du Pont's notebook, "Botanique: Méthode du Jardin des Plantes."

Section 3 fructification placé pres de la racine.

Pilulaire · Pilularia ·

une coque sessile, velue spherique; 4 valves, 4 loges;
renfermant les étamines et les pistils.

Marsilea

une coque ovoïde, portée sur un pedoncule, partagée transversal=
=ement en plusieurs loges, qui renferment les étamines et les pistils.

Classe 2. monocotyledones apetales, étamines attachées
. sous le pistil.

Ordre 1 · les Nayades · Nayades ·

Cal. entier ou decoupé, rarement o. ovaire supere ou infere.
1 – 2 Styles ou Stigm. graines nues ou renfermées dans un
pericarpe. feuilles ordinairement opposées ou verticillées.
Obs. toutes les plantes de cette famille qui est peu naturelle,
croissent dans les eaux.

Volant d'Eau · Myriophyllum ·

fl. monoïques ou hermaphrodites. Cal. 4 div. 4–8 étam. Styl. o.
4 Stigm. 4 noix. (Dicotyledone Goertner)

arrived at its new home at Bergen Point, New Jersey, in January 1800. To this home, with twenty acres of ground, ample space for gardens, they gave the name of Bon Séjour. The colonizing project was soon abandoned because of the highly inflated prices of land created by a decade of speculation, even in the "wild" lands of the frontier regions. The idea of purchasing and landscaping lots in Washington was given up, possibly for the same reason, because property in the capital had been subject to much speculation. Reporting on a trip he took to the new seat of government in August 1800, Victor admired the handsome new buildings that were being erected, but in his opinion the capital city would "look like nothing but a collection of country estates for the next two hundred years."

Victor became an import-export merchant in New York City, and Irénée turned his attention to the soil, improving and enlarging the gardens surrounding their home. Their father was proud of his sons: "Victor is admirable for my business, and he has lots of ideas and wisdom. Irénée is no less good for my gardens; what he has done at Bon Séjour is astonishing." Another member of the family, Mrs. Victor du Pont, an observant lady, saw in what direction her brother-in-law's true inclinations lay: "His tastes are simple: botany, hunting, fishing, rural responsibilities. In sum, all the joys one can find in country living and in a happy household are his." Botany, be it noted, was his first love.

The resources of this happy household, however, were dwindling month by month as various promising enterprises were considered and then rejected in family council. Sometime in the early fall of 1800, it was decided that a black powder factory should be established under Irénée's direction. His experience gained at the Arsenal and at the Essonne mills in the years 1787–1791 equipped him for this undertaking, but it was thought it would be well if he made a return trip to France to acquaint himself with the newer methods and the improved machinery which the Régie des Poudres had adopted during the past ten years.

This he did in January 1801, accompanied on the crossing by Victor, whose mission was to try to acquire more capital for Du Pont (de Nemours) Père, Fils et Compagnie, and to establish more trade contacts for his own commercial business with European merchants. The brothers arrived at LeHavre shortly after several attempts had been made upon the life of the first consul, Napoleon Bonaparte.

Fig. 7 Passport of E. I. du Pont, 1799. Courtesy of Delaware State Archives.

Immigration authorities examined all new arrivals with close scrutiny and carefully checked their passports. Victor, as a merchant, was quickly cleared, but the immigration people were puzzled by the "Botaniste" on Irénée's passport (fig. 7); they had received no instructions from Paris on what to do about botanists entering the country! Irénée, much to his disgust, was told he would be detained until clearance came from the capital. Believing Irénée's time more precious than his own, Victor proposed that they exchange identities and passports, he becoming the detained botanist and Irénée the merchant free to move on. In the midst of some heated Gallic expostulations the immigration officers learned that the brothers were the sons of Pierre Samuel du Pont de Nemours, "a man generally beloved and respected," and, to quote Victor, they changed their minds, "revised their arrêté, and agreed that a Botanist might not be a conspirator."

In Victor's baggage was a small box containing seeds of a hundred different kinds entrusted to him by William Hamilton, gentleman farmer and scientific agriculturist, owner of The Woodlands, an estate on the banks of the Schuylkill River in Philadelphia. Hamilton had asked Victor to offer the seeds, some new and rare, to persons in France who would like to begin an exchange of seeds, plants, and shrubs with him. Victor was given a list of the kinds of things Hamilton in turn would like to have sent to him for propagation on his estate. André Michaux, the French naturalist who had spent the decade 1786–1796 in America was suggested as a likely correspondent, as was André Thouin, director of the Jardin des Plantes, who Hamilton hoped would "enter on a correspondence for the mutual exchange of good offices in the botanic line. . . . You can safely assure him that there is no one in this country better situated or more able to serve him in this respect." Hamilton also asked Victor to obtain for him a catalogue of the plants growing in the gardens at Versailles.

Hamilton subsequently lived up to his promise, but his "good offices in the botanic line" came to be exchanges with the son of Michaux, François André Michaux, like his father a naturalist, whose associations with the du Ponts will be discussed in Chapter III. It may have been Victor who introduced Michaux to Hamilton after the former's arrival in America in 1801. In his book on American trees, *Histoire des arbres forestiers de l'Amérique septen-*

Plate 1 Amphitheater in the Jardin des Plantes where E. I. du Pont attended botanical lectures. Photograph by Hampfler.

Plate 2 Dwarf and espaliered fruit trees at Bois-des-Fossés today. This form of fruit culture, long practiced in France, was adopted in the gardens at Eleutherian Mills. Photographs by Hampfler.

trionale, Michaux describes fine specimens of several kinds of trees which grew in the park of Hamilton's Woodlands estate. Here, for instance, he found the small or dwarf chestnut oak: "I discovered it again at the very doorstep of Philadelphia, in the estate of William Hamilton, where it grows wild."

If the customs agents had examined the "botanist's" sea chest, or portmanteau, they would have found another supply of seeds and seedlings which Irénée was taking to Bois-des-Fossés for the new occupant, his cousin Philippe Harmand, to plant there. Some were also going to M. Bernier, a lawyer and du Pont family friend who had a country place near Egreville, a few miles distant. The supply given to Harmand was of such variety and abundance that Victor, presciently, thought it fitting to enter this cryptic designation of their old home in his journal: BOIS-DES-FOSSÉS. NURSERY OF AMERICAN TREES.

In his conversations with M. Robin, head of the powder mills at Essonne, Irénée learned that both he and Jean Riffault, chief of the Régie des Poudres, were enthusiastic gardeners who would welcome trees and plants of American origin for their gardens. To Bernier at Egreville, Irénée sent off a request asking that he forward to Robin some of the seeds and cuttings that had been left with him. And he promised Robin and Riffault that when he returned to the United States he would send them more seeds of American trees. Robin responded by assuring Irénée that he would be "an eager cultivator of the trees from the beautiful country in which you live."

The following year Robin acknowledged a shipment Irénée had sent in January 1802 (fig. 8), mentioning several trees he was particularly pleased to receive—walnut, oak, beech, and tulip—and which he had planted, "So I hope that our groves will be increased in beauty and utility by the valuable American trees." The chief of the powder works shared Irénée's gift with other amateur gardeners and with the botanists at Fontainebleau and Versailles. In the little park called "Relais de Poste aux Chevaux" at Essonne today there grow a tulip tree, a purple beech, and a very large plane tree, none of which is native to Europe. It is not too great a strain on credulity to suppose that these were grown from the seeds or small trees given to Robin by Irénée in 1801 and 1802.

Riffault planted part of the shipment sent to him on his small estate and gave the rest to the Society of Agriculture and Science of Touraine, thanking Irénée in these words: "It is much to be

Graines envoyées en France en 1802.

	M. Deshayes.	Mme Buonaparte.	M. de Dreux.	M. Michely	M. Thouin	M. Morel	M. Picot La Peyrouse.	M. Robin.	M. Riffault.
Acer Rubrum	1	2	3	4	〃	6	7	8	9.
Andromeda Caliculata	〃	2	3	4	〃	〃	〃	〃	〃.
—— Panicutata	1	2	3	4	〃	6	7	8	9.
—— Racemosa	1	2	3	4	〃	6	7	8	9.
Annona triloba	〃	〃	3	4	〃	〃	〃	〃	〃.
Aralia Spinosa	〃	2	3	4	5	6	7	8	9.
Arbutus ferruginea	〃	2	3	4	5	6	7	〃	〃.
Azalea nudiflora	〃	2	〃	4	〃	〃	〃	〃	〃
—— Viscosa	1	2	3	4	5	6	7	8	9.
Betula Lenta	〃	〃	3	4	〃	6	7	8	9.
Carpinus ostrya	〃	〃	3	4	〃	6	7	8	9.
—— Virginiana	〃	〃	3	4	〃	6	7	8	9.
Ceanothus americanus	〃	2	3	4	5	6	7	8	9.
Celastrus Scandens	1	2	3	4	5	6	7	8	9.
Celtis occidentalis	〃	〃	3	4	〃	〃	〃	8	9.
Cephalanthus occident.	1	2	3	4	〃	6	7	8	9.
Clethra alnifolia	1	2	3	4	〃	6	7	8	9.
Cornus alba	〃	2	〃	〃	5	6	7	〃	〃.
—— alternifolia	〃	2	3	4	〃	6	7	〃	〃.
—— florida	1	2	3	4	5	6	7	8	9.
Cupressus Thuyoides	〃	〃	3	4	〃	6	7	8	9.
Diospyros Virginiana	1	2	3	4	5	6	7	8	9.
—— 4a	〃	〃	〃	〃	5	〃	〃	〃	〃.
Evonimus Semper Vir.	〃	2	〃	4	〃	〃	〃	〃	〃.
Fagus Castanea am.	〃	〃	3	4	5	6	7	8	9.
—— Pumila	〃	2	3	4	5	6	7	8	9.
—— Sylvatica am.	〃	〃	3	4	〃	6	7	8	9.
Fraxinus alba	〃	〃	3	4	〃	6	7	8	9.
—— Nigra	〃	〃	3	4	〃	6	7	8	9.
Gaultheria Rocumb.	〃	〃	〃	4	5	6	7	〃	〃.
Halesia tetraptera	〃	2	3	4	〃	〃	〃	〃	〃.
Hedera quinque folia	〃	2	3	4	5	6	7	〃	〃.
Hibiscus Palustris	1	2	3	4	5	6	7	8	9.
Juglans alba (White nut Hickory)	1	2	3	4	5	6	7	8	9.
—— alba latifolia (Mocker nut Hickory)	1	2	3	4	5	6	7	8	9.
—— alba (Bigest mocker nut Hickory)	〃	〃	〃	〃	5	6	7	8	9.
—— alba ovalis	〃	2	3	4	5	6	7	8	9.
—— alba (Pig nut Hickory)	1	2	3	4	5	6	7	8	9.
—— alba Cordiformis	1	2	3	4	5	6	7	8	9.
—— Nigra	1	2	3	4	5	6	7	8	9.
—— Cinerea	1	2	3	4	〃	6	7	8	9.
Juniperus Virginiana	1	2	3	4	〃	6	7	8	9.
Kalmia latifolia	1	2	3	4	5	6	7	8	9.
Laurus Benzoin	〃	2	3	4	〃	〃	〃	〃	〃
—— Sassafras	1	2	3	4	5	6	7	8	9.
Liquidambar Styraciflua	1	2	3	4	5	6	7	8	9.
Liriodendron tulipifera	1	2	3	4	5	6	7	8	9.
Magnolia glauca	1	2	3	4	5	6	7	8	9.
—— tripetala	〃	2	〃	〃	〃	〃	〃	〃	〃.
Myrica Cerifera	1	2	3	4	5	6	7	8	9.
Nyssa Sylvatica	〃	2	3	4	5	6	7	8	9.
Potentilla fruticosa am.	〃	2	〃	4	〃	6	7	〃	〃.
Prinos Glaber	1	2	3	4	5	6	7	8	9.
—— Verticillatus	1	2	3	4	5	6	7	8	9.
—— 4a	〃	〃	〃	〃	5	6	7	〃	〃.
Prunus Cerasus Virgin.	〃	2	3	4	〃	6	7	8	9.
Pyrola maculata	〃	〃	3	4	5	6	7	〃	〃
Quercus alba	〃	〃	3	4	〃	〃	〃	8	9.
—— alba Palustris	〃	〃	〃	〃	〃	〃	〃	8	9.
—— Nigra	〃	〃	3	4	〃	〃	〃	8	9.
—— Nigra trifida	〃	〃	3	4	〃	〃	〃	8	9.
—— Rubra	〃	〃	3	4	〃	〃	〃	8	9.
—— Rubra Ramosissima	〃	〃	3	4	〃	〃	〃	〃	〃.
—— Phellos angustifol.	〃	〃	3	4	〃	〃	〃	8	9.
—— Phellos Latifolia	〃	〃	〃	〃	〃	〃	〃	8	9.
Rhododendrum maxim.	1	2	3	4	5	6	7	8	9.
Rhus Copallinum	1	2	3	4	〃	6	7	8	9.
—— Rubrum	1	2	3	4	〃	6	7	8	9.
—— typhinum	1	2	3	4	〃	6	7	8	9.
—— toxicodendron	1	2	3	4	〃	6	7	8	9.
Spiraea Crenata	〃	2	3	4	5	6	7	〃	〃.
—— tomentosa	〃	2	3	4	5	6	7	〃	〃.
Staphilaea trifoliata	〃	2	3	4	〃	6	〃	8	9.
Sarracenia purpurea	〃	〃	〃	〃	5	〃	〃	〃	〃
Viburnum Crenatum	1	2	3	4	〃	6	7	8	9.
—— Pyrifolium	1	2	3	4	〃	6	7	8	9.
—— Prunifolium	1	2	3	4	〃	6	7	8	9.

Fig. 9 Packing list of seeds sent to France in 1802 by E. I. du Pont naming recipients and the kinds of seeds they received.

Fig. 8 (opposite page) Alphabetized list of seeds for the above shipment.

wished that our beautiful Touraine, already so rich in fruit trees, should become so in thriving nurseries of ornamental and useful trees. I think that most of the superb American ones will thrive. And you would surely deserve much of your fatherland if you contributed so wisely to the improving and beautifying of one of the most beautiful parts of her territory."

Another recipient of an American tree was a M. Pitra, a Parisian friend of du Pont de Nemours, who thanked Irénée for the gift, telling him he had planted it in a small garden on the Isle Louviers and had baptized it "Dupont."

Victor, too, was drawn further into this botanical exchange. In March 1801 he was the guest of a M. Tochon who had a country seat near Boulogne. His host, wrote Victor, was "very fond of botanics and has a garden full of exotic plants. He made me promise him some seeds from America." Persons in high places, one none other than the first consul's wife, Mme. Josephine Bonaparte, conveyed word to du Pont that she too would like to have some American seeds. All that Irénée had brought with him had already been distributed and planted, but he promised Mme. Bonaparte that in the autumn after he had returned to America he would send an assortment to her (fig. 9).

CHAPTER III

The Gardens of the Republic

One single variety of tree suitable for shipbuilding or any other important industry, if introduced and cultivated in France, would be an indestructible source of wealth and one that would always increase in value.

E. I. du Pont to Picot La Péyrouse, 1802

WHILE in Paris during the early months of 1801, possibly on one of his visits to the Jardin des Plantes, Irénée heard the disquieting news that the French government was about to close down two nurseries, or pépinières, it had maintained in America since 1786, one in Goose Creek Parish ten miles north of Charleston, South Carolina, and the other in Bergen's Wood near Hackensack, New Jersey. These Jardins de la République had been established by the naturalist André Michaux to grow plants, shrubs, and trees and to provide seeds of American botanical and horticultural species, all of which were sent to France for distribution and propagation throughout the country; from France he had imported many plant materials native to Europe for cultivation in the American gardens. In his own explorations throughout the eastern United States Michaux discovered *Magnolia cordata* and *Magnolia macrophylla*, and he introduced crape myrtle, *Lagerstroemia indica*, into southern gardens. The Charleston gardener was Mathias Kin, and the gardener at Hackensack was Pierre Paul Saulnier, formerly of the Jardin des Plantes, who had come to the United States with Michaux.

The Hackensack nursery was not easily accessible to travelers unfamiliar with the back roads of eastern New Jersey (fig. 10), as the Reverend Manasseh Cutler discovered when he tried to locate it in mid-July of 1787 with the intent of calling upon Michaux to learn about the Jardin de la République. Vexed at being misdirected and having to journey farther than he anticipated, he arrived at the garden only to find neither Michaux nor Saulnier there to greet him;

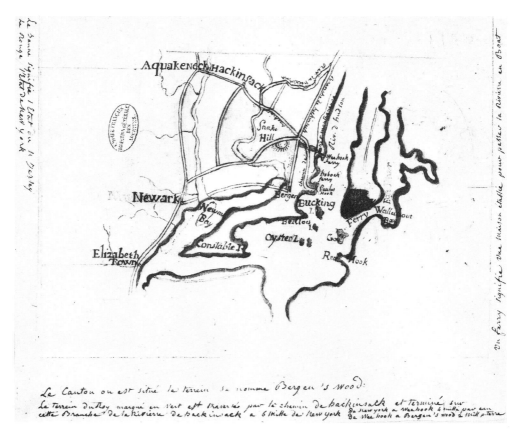

Fig. 10 Rough map by André Michaux showing location of the garden of the French government in the Bergen's Wood–Hackensack area. Courtesy of Bibliothèque Nationale.

they had gone to South Carolina. Guided by a stolid garden laborer, Reverend Cutler was not at all impressed by what he saw:

There was no order of beauty in the gardens, the soil remarkably sandy and poor, the situation wretched and the way to it as bad as can well be conceived. Of all places in America, this would have been the very last I should have thought of for such a purpose. What could induce Michaux to fix down in this awful, gloomy, lonely, miserable spot, is beyond my power to conceive. I was never more disappointed and regretted the pains I had taken to see the ill taste and judgment of this Botanical Frenchman.

Michaux had selected this spot because it possessed six different types of soil, a diversity permitting the cultivation of a variety of dissimilar plants and trees (fig. 11).

Despite this unflattering view of it (possibly Cutler was unaware that it was hardly a year under cultivation), the nurseries at Hackensack and Charleston continued for ten years, until Michaux returned to France, to stock the gardens of France with growing things indigenous to the North American continent; in turn, Saulnier and Kin planted in the gardens under their care many trees and shrubs which were sent over from Europe. Those items grown in the 111-acre Charleston garden usually went to the southern, warmer regions of France; those from the 29-acre Hackensack garden to the northern, colder areas.

The Baron de Palisot de Beauvois, a French naturalist visiting the United States during the years 1793–1798, visited the Charleston garden and sent a report of it to French Consul General Philippe Joseph Létombe in Philadelphia. France, he said, was being enriched by the plant materials Michaux was sending there from Charleston; they "can only contribute to the splendor of the country, to the comfort, well-being, and general advantage of its inhabitants." Beauvois favored enlarging the garden so that rather than a few of each item being sent to France to become curiosities, sufficient quantities could be exported to allow widespread planting.

The soil in the garden was good for growing things—a sand mixed with shell deposits and decayed vegetation found in the coastal areas of South Carolina and Georgia. The seeds and plants that Michaux had brought back from his trips into the interior were carefully nurtured and looked healthy. Others that might not have survived being transported a great distance had been propagated by being grafted onto similar plants.

Beauvois's sole criticism of the garden was that plants natural to colder climates could not be cultivated there. Despite the special care that Michaux daily lavished upon them, either the seeds did not grow, or they died shortly after germination. Apparently unaware of the existence of the Hackensack garden, he suggested to Létombe that a second Jardin de la République be established in the vicinity of Philadelphia where plants native to the north could be grown for transplanting to the colder parts of France. Both gardens, he concluded, could become much more valuable if they were made the

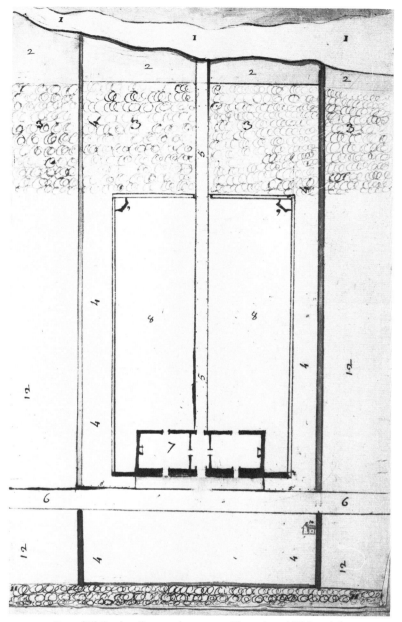

1. Cromakill Creek, tributary of the Hackensack River
2. Meadow land
3. Cedar swamps
4. Bounds of garden
5. Avenue of trees
6. Hackensack Road
7. Floor plan of Michaux's house
8. Garden of valuable plants
9. Greenhouses for non-hardy trees
10. Gardener's house
11. Rolling woodlands
12. Neighboring private lands

Fig. 11 Sketch by André Michaux of the garden of the French government in New Jersey. Courtesy of Bibliothèque Nationale.

repositories of all branches of the natural sciences of North America —birds, insects, minerals and animals—which, like plants and seeds, would also be sent to his home country, so that "soon the opossum, the raccoon, etc., would be seen there." The Charleston garden was in very good order, he reported; "It cannot be put in better hands than those of the zealous and industrious Citizen Michaux."

Michaux kept careful record of the shipments, noting that between 1786 and 1792 sixty thousand plants, six thousand trees, and ninety boxes of seeds had been sent to the king's agents, M. d'Angiviller and the Abbé Nolin, for planting in the royal gardens and in an experimental garden Michaux had established at Louis XVI's direction at Rambouillet for this purpose. The king's physician, Louis Guillaume Lemonnier, also a professor of botany, planted his garden at Montreuil, near Versailles, with American trees, shrubs, and medicinal plants sent to him by Michaux.

After Michaux's departure from the United States in 1796, the gardens were neglected by the home government; orders from France dwindled, and the gardeners went unpaid for a number of years. As a consequence, to compensate themselves, Kin and Saulnier assumed a quasi-proprietorship and seem to have operated the gardens as private nurseries. (Michaux died on the island of Madagascar in 1802 while on a scientific and collecting expedition led by Captain Thomas Nicolas Baudin.)

Du Pont learned while in France that Jean Chaptal, minister of the Interior, whose department had jurisdiction over the gardens, was sending the son of the man who had founded them, François André Michaux, to America late in 1801, to wind up affairs, settle accounts with Kin and Saulnier, and dispose of the two *pépinières*. The younger Michaux was not a stranger to the United States, for he had accompanied his father in 1786 and lived with him near Charleston for ten years; hence he was familiar with the gardens and the work carried on there. Irénée considered the abolition of the gardens a short-sighted measure dictated by false economy, noting that the yearly cost of maintaining them was trifling, about twelve hundred francs, compared with the benefits to be derived from the continued introduction and propagation in France "of useful and curious plants from the new continent."

Kin and Saulnier somehow came to know that du Pont was concerned about the pending demise of the gardens in their keeping (the du Pont home at Bergen Point was only a few miles away from the *pépinière* in Bergen's Wood) and they wrote to Irénée, asking that he use his influence, and that of his father, with friends and associates who might persuade the government to continue rather than dispose of the gardens. Kin offered to rent the Charleston garden or to make an arrangement whereby he could maintain it for the Ecole de Botanique at Strasbourg. Irénée approved the suggestions, just so France would benefit from what was grown, and he advised Kin to present his proposals directly to the younger Michaux as soon as he arrived in Charleston. He assured Kin that he had written to friends in France entreating their assistance and that he had also been in touch with Louis André Pichon, chargé d'affaires of the French Republic in New York. But Pichon would promise nothing; he preferred to let the matter rest until he had discussed it with Michaux.

Michaux arrived in Charleston in early December 1801, and one of his earliest letters was addressed to Pierre Samuel du Pont de Nemours at Bon Séjour, telling him that his mission was to dispose of the Jardins de la République. Illness detained him in Charleston for a time. He was surprised, when taking up residence at the garden, near what later became Ten Mile Station, to find that a superb collection of trees and plants had survived, even through several years' neglect, and he recognized many plantings dating from the years when he and his father had lived there (fig. 12).

Michaux's declaration of his intent to terminate them spurred Irénée to launch a "Save the Gardens" campaign. He wrote letters to a number of persons influential in French scientific circles and to others who had contacts with officials who, he believed, could gain the ear of the minister of the interior. With each letter there usually went a collection of seeds, plants, and small trees. Among those whose aid he solicited were Picot La Péyrouse, mayor of the city of Toulouse and director of that city's botanical gardens; J. F. Nicholas Morel, botanical physician of Besançon, author of *L'art des jardins dans la nature,* and who had recently published *Tableau de l'Ecole de botanique du Jardin des plantes;* M. Des Hayes, head of the legal bureau of the Interior Department; M. Robin and M. Riffault of the Régie des Poudres, who, as previously noted, had shared their first shipments from Irénée with the gardeners at Versailles and Fontainebleau. He solicited the intervention of André Thouin, di-

Fig. 12 Specimen of *Pinckneya pubens,* Georgia bark, found growing on the site of the French government garden near Charleston, S.C. Courtesy of Charleston Museum.

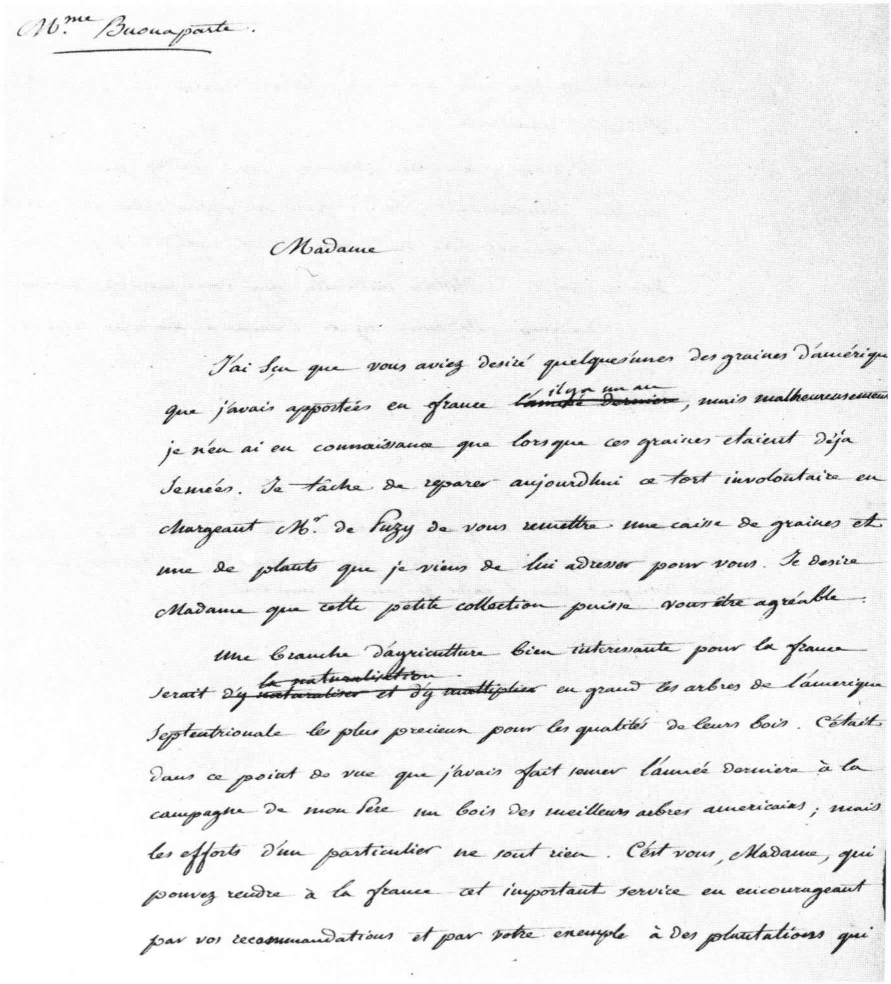

Mme Buonaparte.

Madame

J'ai Sçu que vous aviez desiré quelquesunes des graines d'amérique que j'avais apportées en france ~~l'année dernière~~ il y a un an, mais malheureusement je n'en ai eu connaissance que lorsque ces graines etaient déja Semées. Je tache de reparer aujourdhui ce tort involontaire en chargeant Mr. de Fuzy de vous remettre une caisse de graines et une de plants que je viens de lui adresser pour vous. Je desire Madame que cette petite collection puisse vous être agréable.

Une branche d'agriculture bien interessante pour la france serait d'y ~~naturaliser et d'y multiplier~~ la naturalisation en grand les arbres de l'amerique Septentrionale les plus precieux pour les qualités de leurs bois. C'était dans ce point de vue que j'avais fait semer l'année dernière à la campagne de mon père un bois des meilleurs arbres americains; mais les efforts d'un particulier ne sont rien. C'est vous, Madame, qui pouvez rendre à la france cet important service en encourageant par vos recommandations et par votre exemple à des plantations qui

Fig. 13 Rough draft of E. I. du Pont's letter to Mme. Bonaparte.

rector of the Jardin des Plantes; his cousin, Philippe Harmand at Bois-des-Fossés, who was a government official; Alexandre Brongniart, scientist and director of the Museum of Natural History; Minister of the Interior Chaptal, the key figure in the issue; and Mme. Bonaparte herself.

The letter to the First Lady of France was skillfully worded, de-

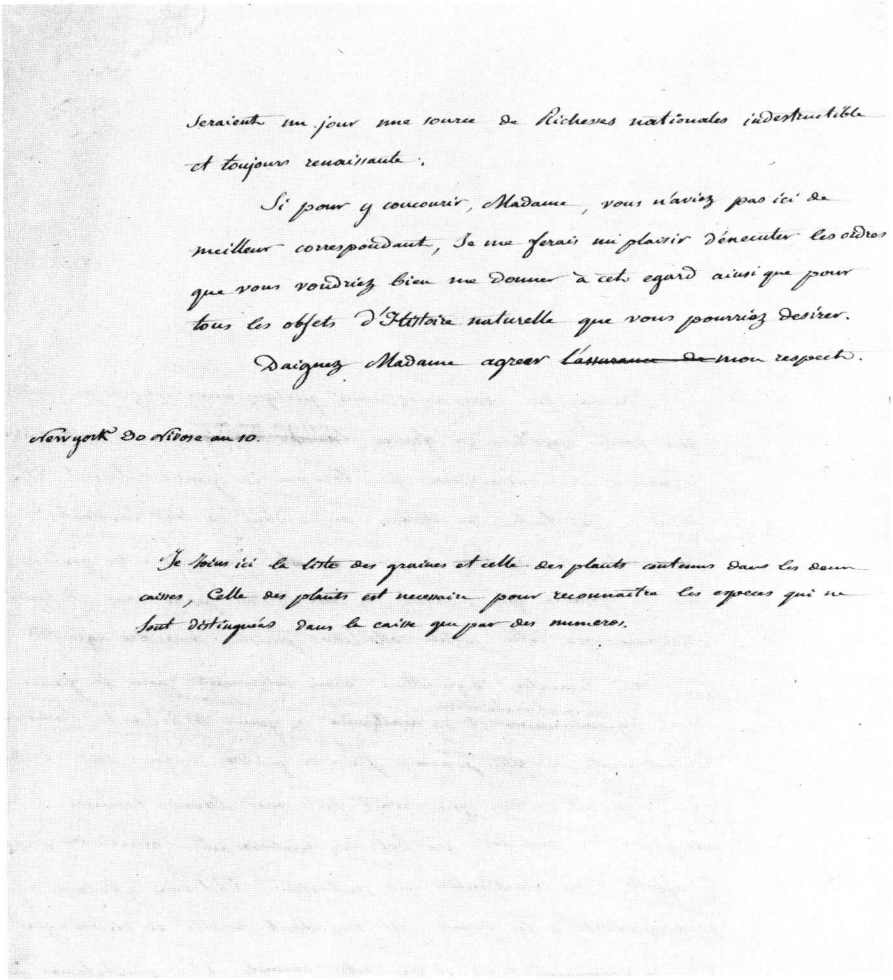

[handwritten letter in French]

Seraient un jour une source de Richesses nationales indestructible
et toujours renaissante.

Si pour y concourir, Madame, vous n'aviez pas ici de
meilleur correspondant, Je me ferais un plaisir d'exécuter les ordres
que vous voudriez bien me Donner à cet egard ainsi que pour
tous les objets d'Histoire naturelle que vous pourriez Desirer.

Daignez Madame agréer l'assurance ~~de mon~~ respect.

Newyork 30 nivôse an 10.

Je Joins ici la liste des graines et celle des plants contenus dans les deux
caisses, Celle des plants est necessaire pour reconnaitre les especes qui ne
sont distinguées dans la caisse que par des numeros.

signed to persuade her to become a patroness of botanical exchange
between the Old and New Worlds (fig. 13). Her direct assistance
to save the Jardins de la République would be sought in person by
Bureaux de Pusy, du Pont's stepbrother-in-law and a close friend of
the Marquis de Lafayette. De Pusy, who had come to America a
short time before the du Ponts, was returning to France in January

1802, and to him Irénée entrusted two boxes containing 150 botanical items for delivery to Mme. Bonaparte. This was Irénée's letter that accompanied the gift:

I was told that you wanted some of the American seeds that I took to France a year ago, but unfortunately the message did not reach me till after the seeds were sown. I am trying to atone for my involuntary mistake by sending you a box of seeds and one of plants. I hope, Madame, that this little collection may please you. A branch of agriculture that would be very valuable to France would be the acclimatizing on a large scale of the trees of North America whose wood is most precious. For that reason I had a grove of some of the best American trees sowed on my Father's estate last year, but the efforts of one person amount to nothing. You, Madame, can do a great service to France by encouraging, both by advice and example, plantations that will some day be a source of indestructible wealth that will always increase. If for that purpose, Madame, you have no better correspondent here, it would give me great pleasure to execute any order you might send me, in this matter or in any department of natural history.

Acknowledgment by Mme. Bonaparte came to du Pont through his cousin Philippe Harmand at Bois-des-Fossés. She was very pleased with the plants and seeds, and they were being planted in the gardens at Malmaison, the "Trianon Consulaire" in the western suburbs of Paris (plate 3) to which the Bonapartes recently had moved. At Malmaison Josephine was becoming the patroness of botanists, nurserymen, and hybridizers. One of her special projects was to plant in her gardens all the known species and varieties of roses, then about 250 in number. In French floriculture her patronage ushered in an era that has been called "The Renaissance of the Rose." By coincidence her rose gardener was named André du Pont, considered France's first rosarian. When home from campaigns and the halls of government, Napoleon enjoyed his respites at Malmaison. Second to the battlefield, said his secretary Bourrienne, Napoleon was happiest when strolling through Josephine's gardens: "Nowhere, except on the field of battle, did I ever see Bonaparte more happy than in the gardens of Malmaison."

A second box sent to Harmand was shared by him with Mme. Antoine Lavoisier, widow of the chemist and long a friend of the du Pont family, who was delighted to receive the items for planting at her home at Orgelet. Harmand planted his portion and promised

Fig. 14 The conservatory at Malmaison, from a watercolor by Auguste Garneray, 1810.
Courtesy of Musée National du Château de Malmaison.

Irénée that when he next visited France he would show him a "bit of America" at his old home at Bois-des-Fossés. Seven years later, at a time when Irénée was contemplating a trip home, Harmand wrote, "I have a pretty garden. Among the trees growing there are two that I am fonder of than of any others—a catalpa and a walnut that you gave me; I have had the greatest happiness in seeing them grow."

For the specimens he sent to La Péyrouse, mayor of Toulouse, and director of its botanical gardens, Irénée apologized for the rather poor quality of the seeds: 1801 had not been a good growing year but next year's shipment would be better, he promised. Most of the seeds sent to the mayor had come from the Jardin de la République at Hackensack, a valuable establishment threatened with destruction, added Irénée. He entreated La Péyrouse to ask his friends in Paris to do all they could to prevent this. His father had written to the Institut National, hoping that the prestige of that respected learned society might stay the hand of the government. The Institut had sent a commission to call upon the minister of the Interior, but to no avail. The gardens, in the eyes of French officials, had been of little service in recent years and were too costly to maintain.

But Irénée confided to La Péyrouse that he did not believe this to be the real reason for the government's intent to close the gardens. Some proprietors of large nurseries in France did not want the Republic's American gardens to compete with them. They imported a great variety of American stock from commercial growers in the United States which they sold at high prices. This had never been openly stated, but du Pont was certain such was the real source of the opposition. However, Michaux could not close the gardens until he had settled accounts with the gardeners Kin and Saulnier and had paid them their back wages. It would take time to do this because he had brought no funds with him; the forced respite would give the true friends of botany time to increase their efforts to save the gardens.

Irénée informed La Péyrouse that every year Germany, England, and Denmark ordered sizable shipments of seeds and plants from America for which they paid high prices. (Possibly du Pont knew that Humphry Marshall, naturalist and nurseryman, from his gardens and woods near West Chester, Pennsylvania, had been supplying English estate owners and such worthies as Dr. John Fothergill

Plate 3 Malmaison. Photograph by Hampfler.

Plate 4 Vauréal, home of François André Michaux. Photograph by Hampfler.

and Sir Joseph Banks of the Royal Society for over thirty years.) He asked La Péyrouse, rhetorically,

Is it not deplorable that France should be behind them and, instead of taking part in a competition so important for the improvement of agriculture, she herself should destroy the very thing that gives her an advantage over other countries? One single variety of tree suitable for shipbuilding or any other important industry, if introduced and cultivated in France, would be an indestructible source of wealth and one that would always increase in value.

Du Pont apologized for the length of his letter, but the subject deserved it, "and my interest in the sciences, and particularly in botany, makes me feel a deep interest."

About this time a Joseph de Dreux, a Frenchman visiting the United States, met du Pont in Philadelphia. Whether he was a botanist, a landscape architect, or a commercial nurseryman is not clear. Learning of Irénée's zeal to have American species propagated in France, he requested him to put together a collection to be shipped to him after he had returned home. Judging from the extent of his request, de Dreux seems to have assumed that du Pont was in the nursery business rather than busily engaged in establishing a black powder plant. He asked du Pont to send him the seeds of all kinds of laurels; of *Magnolia grandiflora, M. glauca, M. longifolia, M. acuminata, M. tripetala;* of tulip trees, sugar maples, ash trees, oak trees, nuts, pines (particularly the southern pine), firs, red cedars, Virginia cedar, Louisiana cypress, Canadian birch, and mulberries. He also wanted all the seeds, nuts, bulbs, onions, and roots of trees, bushes, shrubs, "indigenous and exotic plants that are to be found on the different parts of the American continent." Obviously du Pont could not take the time to collect this large assortment, but he did fill part of the order, possibly with some assistance from Kin and Saulnier, for de Dreux acknowledged receiving an "instructive list which has given me infinite pleasure." If de Dreux was stocking a nursery, his request could have been much more appropriately sent a few years later to Lewis and Clark to be filled by them while on their transcontinental exploring, mapping, and botanizing expedition instigated by President Thomas Jefferson.

Irénée counted on Thouin, director of the Jardin des Plantes, for strong support in his efforts to save the Charleston and Hackensack gardens. In his letter that went along with the "botanical" box, Irénée identified himself as a former student: "Botany, which I began to study in your school, has been a great pleasure to me in this country where its forms are so new to me; but I wish that the time I am able to devote to it could be more useful to France by helping to introduce and cultivate the valuable and beautiful plants of this continent." He asked Thouin to let him know what seeds and plants he would like sent from America. Du Pont had checked the catalogue of the Jardin des Plantes and had not found in it a curious plant that grew in the American swamps, *Sarracenia purpurea,* the native pitcher plant, so he was taking the liberty of sending some roots of it to Thouin. If Thouin wished to reciprocate, Irénée would send him a list of the European plants and fruit trees that did not grow in this country which Irénée would like to introduce. For the director he reviewed Michaux's mission, enumerated all the reasons why it should not succeed— "A real source of wealth is to be annihilated for a contemptible economy of twelve hundred francs a year"—and appealed to him to use all his influence with the proper officials to have the gardens preserved.

This was the tenor of all of du Pont's "botanical" letters to France in the early months of 1802, a very busy time for him, for he was traveling widely to find the most suitable place to erect his black powder factory. Of all his correspondents, the most promising response came from the mayor of Toulouse, who sent along some plants and trees from the city gardens which he directed. La Péyrouse had written many letters, using extracts from du Pont's letters to him, to friends in Paris, but no one had replied. He had discussed the preservation of the French botanic gardens in America with two officials of the Jardin des Plantes, and he had presented a memoir on the matter to Chaptal, minister of the Interior, but that gentleman had made no acknowledgment. He asked du Pont to favor him with some conifers, some seeds of *l'érable à sucre* (the sugar maple), and some bulbs of *Lilium superbum.*

J. F. Nicholas Morel, the botanical physician at Besançon, expressed a desire to begin a regular exchange of botanical items with Irénée and sent him a small assortment accompanied by instructions for planting and use. This was the shipment, with Morel's annotation of each item:

Convolvulus tricolor. A very pretty bindweed. It should be sown in hot frames in April or in the open ground in May and used for clumps or borders.

Larkspur Julien. Should be sown in April or May in open ground mixed with mould.

Larkspur, double. Large and very pretty. This is from the garden of the Tuileries where they are superb. Planted like the preceding.

Xeranthemum annuum. An annual that bears quantities of beautiful flowers. Sown in rich open ground in May.

Campanula medium. Two varieties. To be sown in damp ground in the shade.

Morning-glory, purple. Very beautiful climbing plant bearing a multitude of purple flowers. Should be sown in May near trellises and arbors.

Oenothera odorata. A plant that bears large yellow flowers with the perfume of orange flowers. To be sown in open ground in May or earlier.

Trees

Mimosa julibrissin—Constantinople acacia. A greenhouse plant. Superb, growing to a height of 25 feet and more. To be sown in a hot frame and brought in for the winter.

Sophora japonica. Tree much sought after in Paris, which bears green branches that grow to a great height and which lives in the open air in winter. Should be sown in ordinary soil mixed with peat mould.

Botanical Plants

Anthyllis barba-jovis. Beautiful decorative bush which grows to four or five feet. Should be sown in hot frames and taken in for the winter.

Justicia peruviana. A beautiful plant whose flowers are pink mixed with a little white. To be sown in hotbeds or frames. To be kept in a warm greenhouse in winter.

Crotalaria. An absolutely botanical plant. Rather pretty. Yellow flowers in spikes. Sow in hot frames or warm greenhouse.

Hedysarum vespertilio. A superb and very interesting plant with leaves of unusual form and color. Sow in warm greenhouse in peat mould mixed with one quarter ordinary soil.

Morel promised to send some chestnuts, and he offered to send the catalogue of his gardens from which Irénée should select whatever he wished. These items were received while the du Ponts were still living at Bon Séjour, near Hackensack, but some were soon transplanted to the new home close by Brandywine Creek in New

Castle County, Delaware, when Irénée settled there with his family in mid-July of 1802. In November of that year his brother Victor also sent a supply of trees to the Brandywine home from Bon Séjour in the custody of a German gardener who was to remain and work for Irénée.

We believe Irénée's correspondents in France provided him with the beginnings of the orchard which he planted on his property that soon came to be called Eleutherian Mills. Among his papers is a tree list and the plan of an orchard for nearly five hundred trees—peach, pear, apple, plum, and cherry. The peach trees were of twenty-nine varieties, a few being 'Très Belle Pêche,' 'Pêche rouge,' 'Pêche à larges feuilles,' 'Early Red Cheek,' 'Admirable,' and 'Non Pareille.' There were forty-one different pear trees, the names of some being 'Cuisse Madame,' 'Martin sec,' 'Orange musquée,' 'Epine d'hiver,' 'Colmar,' and 'Sucre vert.' The different varieties of apple trees were twenty-six in number, some of them named 'Calville blanc d'hiver,' 'Reinette franche,' 'Summer Pippin,' 'Late Red Streak,' and 'Uncle Jacob's Sweet.' There were seven varieties of plum trees, including 'Mirabelle,' 'Gros Monsieur,' and 'St. Catherine.' Eleven varieties of cherries were planted, 'Griotte d'Allemagne,' 'Montmorency,' 'Gros Gobet,' and 'Cerisier de la Toussaint' being a few of them.

Another possible source of the plantings at du Pont's new home was the French garden at Hackensack. Saulnier sent him lists of the plants and seeds he could furnish. What were not planted at Eleutherian Mills were no doubt repacked and sent to Irénée's correspondents in France. But not all the boxes sent overseas contained botanical items. Irénée's curiosity ranged over many fields of natural history; he was an avid collector. A box of butterflies was sent to the director of the Museum of Natural History in Paris, Alexandre Brongniart. When Irénée learned later that the butterflies had arrived in damaged condition, he promised to replace them. This would not be difficult, he wrote Brongniart, for Delaware, where he now lived, would provide "birds and insects of greater variety and more beautiful." Whatever time he could spend away from his business would be devoted to natural history research. With this letter went a box of stuffed birds, the taxidermy having been done by Charles Dalmas, Irénée's brother-in-law, who was also something of an artist.

Shortly before his father returned to France in the late spring of 1802, Irénée heard the encouraging news that Michaux had received instructions not to close the French gardens at Hackensack and Charleston. Chaptal, minister of the Interior, had considered the remonstrances protesting such action, noting especially the observations of Pierre Samuel du Pont de Nemours and the stand of the Institut National on the matter. For the present Michaux would limit himself to straightening out the accounts of Saulnier and Kin, and the gardens would be continued until further word was received from France. Michaux was directed to consult with "Citoyen du Pont" when reviewing the gardeners' accounts. It is clear that Chaptal meant Pierre Samuel, but as the senior du Pont was then about to leave the country, whatever was done in concert with Michaux was certainly done by Irénée. The latter realized Chaptal's orders constituted only a reprieve, not an assurance that the gardens would be permanently maintained. But he was now more confident, for his father would soon be speaking to the French authorities in person, and "Bon Papa" could be eloquent, persuasive, and influential.

During the first year of repatriation in his homeland, the elder du Pont had numerous other matters to occupy his mind and his time. His letters to his sons in America had little to say about the French gardens or botany in general, but after being entertained by Mme. Bonaparte at Malmaison in July 1802, he informed Irénée that the wife of the first consul had again expressed a wish that some more trees and seeds be sent to her from America—it would be well if Irénée made a regular shipment each year, sending things at a suitable season for their immediate planting upon arrival in France. In November 1802, the father shipped a large quantity of Lyons chestnuts to Victor in New York for distribution among the family and friends. A number were marked to go to "our dear Irénée at Thunders Mill, at whose expense I make these gifts—as if I were a Prince or Emperor, most generous with the possessions of others. I will send you more from Bois-des-Fossés." Victor was quick to urge his brother to eschew the name Thunders Mill for his new Brandywine powder-making establishment—"rechristen it, for if a letter comes to you by post your Quakers will be horrified."

Renewing his career in French public life, giving what aid he could to the struggling enterprises of his two sons in America, and looking after other family matters were the father's principal concerns. He had managed to gain an audience with Chaptal shortly after his return to France, and he had offered some suggestions about the future of the government gardens in America. Chaptal had promised to consider his proposals and to write to Irénée with definite instructions at a later time. Du Pont senior, adroit in the subtleties of innuendo, reminded Chaptal that Mme. Bonaparte had requested some American plants and that his predecessor in the Interior ministry had always seen to it that she had the first choice of all new shipments arriving from abroad for planting at her beloved Malmaison.

After a year went by with no further word from his father on the subject, Irénée reminded him that the fate of the gardens was still in abeyance. Pessimistically, he cautioned, "I am afraid that all our efforts have only made one more enemy for you in the person of the dealer in France who is eager for the destruction of the gardens." Irénée had heard that France was limiting its import of American seeds to sixty pounds a year, a woefully inadequate amount:

Sixty pounds of seeds of different American trees to be sent each year for the entire supply of the Republic is not even enough for the botanical schools of all the Departments and would do nothing toward naturalizing the valuable varieties and restocking the forests—the only point of view from which the Garden is worthy of the Government's consideration.

Should the gardens be closed, Irénée told his father that he would make himself responsible for seeing that shipments of plants and seeds would be sent to France annually to replace what had formerly come from the "National Gardens" in America. At his new domicile "in the midst of the forests" bordering Brandywine Creek, this would be an easy task. Then, looking ahead, should the powder business fail and he return to France, he noted, "By these shipments and some successful work with plants and trees I may make for myself a position in France, and some day in the future secure a place in the Administration of Forestry." This was written when du Pont was encountering exasperating delays and difficulties in building his mills and his home. There is no doubt that he was then in a despairing, pessimistic mood. Probably, if he had not been committed to the powder venture he would have been strongly tempted to abandon it and to follow a career in botany and horticulture.

The final decision of the French government on the gardens was negative: they were to be closed, but not before Michaux had made a generous selection of their contents and had Saulnier send them off to France. He also set some things aside for Irénée. The Charleston garden passed into the custody of the Agricultural Society of Charleston and is today part of the Charleston airport. The site is memorialized by a stone marker placed there in 1954 by the Garden Club of Charleston. A botanist who visited the garden site in June 1910 found the following trees which he believed had been growing there at the time Irénée had tried to persuade the French government to retain its ownership of the garden: *Magnolia grandiflora,* live oaks, post oaks, water oaks, southern sugar maples, cedars, red birches, white hickories, sweet gums, and red buckeyes; along with hazel nuts, dogwoods, hollies, waxberry, white-leaved blackberry, dewberry, and Jersey tea. What remained of these disappeared with the building of the airport in the 1940s. The Hackensack garden was leased to Saulnier for a number of years and then came to be owned outright by him. Locally it became known as the "Frenchman's Garden." As late as 1809 he was sending materials to the now Empress Josephine Bonaparte for planting in the imperial gardens. Descendants of Saulnier, well along in years in the 1880s, remembered shipments being made to France from their grandfather's garden back in the 1830s. A memorial to Saulnier was erected by the Torrey Botanical Club on the site of his garden near the end of the century, when the property was converted into the Macpelah Cemetery.

Du Pont's diligent efforts to save the Jardins de la République had proved of no avail. Yet he had publicized and had achieved a greater recognition of the benefits to be gained by botanical exchange between France and his newly adopted country. It may have been this service that won him election to the Agricultural Society of Seine and Oise, Versailles, in October 1802. The officers of that society urged him to maintain a regular correspondence with them so that American species could be made known to the society's amateur gardeners and that their gardens might be enriched by his shipments.

His father's efforts, too, should not be overlooked, for in addition to what has already been said in this regard, "Papa" also submitted several lengthy memoranda to the Department of the Interior in which he cogently set forth his son's views and pleaded that the gardens be continued as sources of the first order providing new botanical and horticultural wealth to France. In a memoir titled

"Sur les Forêts," du Pont reviewed briefly the depletion of France's forests since the time of William the Conqueror. They, as well as coastal dunes and parts of Gascony, Berry, and Brittany, would benefit by having planted on them the excellent, diverse types of forest trees from the American gardens. Saulnier, the New Jersey gardener, he told Interior Minister Chaptal, had been very loyal and had stuck to his post for a number of years without compensation, despite attractive offers to assume the management of private estates, one of which had been tendered by Aaron Burr, vice-president of the United States.

CHAPTER IV

The New Home

When I began building my establishment here it was like settling in
the back country, no road, no decent house, no garden. You are aware,
my friend, that being without a garden was the greatest deprivation;
and it is the first thing that occupied my time.

E. I. du Pont to Louis Lelieur, 1803

A MORE immediate and happier consequence of Irénée's losing
struggle to save the Gardens of the Republic was the planting
of the garden and orchard at Eleutherian Mills with many things
sent from France (fig. 15). Soon after he moved his family into the
new home, he begged his father to send him some seeds. "You will
realize how forlorn it is to live in the country and to have no garden,
no fruit for the children." He suggested to "Papa" that he call upon
André Thouin at the Jardin des Plantes and ask him for some
kitchen garden seeds and, above all, some flower seeds. Irénée had
sent Thouin some American seeds a year earlier, so he might wish
to reciprocate. And perhaps Thouin could also furnish some small
fruit trees, preferably cherries, pears, and plums.

A family friend of the du Ponts was Louis Lelieur, a Frenchman
who had lived a few years in America but had returned to France
where subsequently he became director of the gardens at St. Cloud.
Under the Bourbon monarchy he had been in charge of all the royal
parks, gardens, and nurseries. In 1802 Lelieur proposed to Irénée
that they establish a seed business in Paris, specializing in plant materials from the United States. It was an opportune time because
"here no one is concerned with affairs of state, everybody is concerned with agriculture, it is the rage." Irénée turned down the offer
but sent Lelieur a botanical package with an invitation to exchange
garden items. Lelieur responded to the invitation most enthusiasti-
cally:

It is a real pleasure to prove to you that you are right in counting on me
to fill your garden with good things. If Le Havre [under British block-

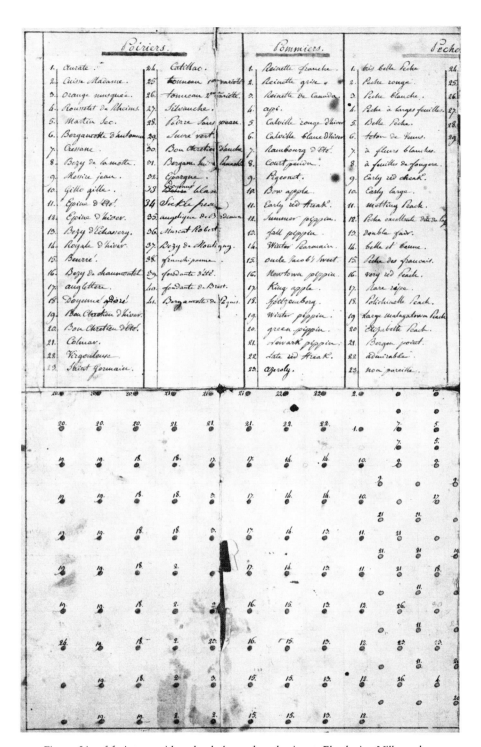

Fig. 15 List of fruit trees with orchard plan and garden insert, Eleutherian Mills, probably 1804.

Cerisiers.		Pruniers.		Suplément.	
				Pommiers.	
Limon.	1.	Griotte de hollande.	1.	Reine claude.	
Pine apple.	2.	Griotte d'Allemagne.	2.	Reine claude violette.	24. Anis.
Hermeille.	3.	mont morency.	3.	monsieur hatif.	25. Seck no further.
Blood.	4.	anglais. hative.	4.	Gros monsieur.	26. Mousseron pippin.
Large White.	5.	anglaise.	5.	Mirabelle.	
Algarine winter.	6.	Gros gobet.	6.	Perdrigon violet.	
	7.	Cerise de la toussaint.	7.	St. Catherine.	
	8.	Royal Mary duck.			
	9.	guigne poutrelle.			
	10.	Bigareau à gros fruit.			
	11.	Blanche à gros fruit.			

ade] were open I would send you ten times as many trees. You will find the vegetable and flower seeds with the trees. I will see that you get all that is possible—I cannot promise more. I do not give up hope of the success of our exchange of seeds. We can accomplish much if we succeed.

Lelieur's sizable shipment consisted of 185 fruit trees—pear, apple, plum, cherry—16 grapevines, 4 nut trees, 2 black mulberry trees, 3 medlar trees, 3 "peach apricots" [nectarines?], some small linden trees, packages of raspberries and some apple grafts, an assortment of rose bushes, and some lavender and violets for the ladies of the household. Mrs. du Pont, who had lamented the absence of a garden to cultivate when first arriving on the Brandywine, was delighted with this abundance, and Irénée was pleased that he would soon be able to provide their children with fresh fruit from the family orchard. He had already begun the orchard, in the early winter of 1802, with a number of peach and cherry trees sent from Bon Séjour and from the orchard of Charles Preudhomme, a Bergen Point neighbor; though late in the season, he had planted them hoping some would survive. The orchard was planted to the west and south of the garden, which was at the front of the house and across from the road that led to the barn and stables. But Irénée regretted the necessity of cutting down some large hardwood trees in order to clear the land for planting.

Du Pont acknowledged Lelieur's generous gift:

When I began building my establishment here it was like settling in the back country, no road, no decent house, no garden. You are aware, my friend that being without a garden was the greatest deprivation; and it is the first thing that occupied my time. I have already planted a hundred excellent peach trees. . . . You cannot realize how prized the good fruits of Europe are in the midst of our woods.

He made a special request that Lelieur send him some young pear trees of the best species, grafted on quinces, for quenouilles planting, training them to grow in the shape of a cone or distaff by tying down the branches. This was written in early August 1803, at the time the family was moving from the small house near the stream which they had occupied for a year into the new larger house on the ridge of land overlooking the powder mills.

Lelieur's request of Irénée was extensive and his packing instructions explicit. He would like some small apple trees, peaches—

"those that are red inside and cling to the stone"—some red and white raspberries, and some white maize. Of decorative plants and woodland trees he wanted the seeds of four types of andromeda, three of azalea, five of laurel, six of magnolia, five of pine, three of ash, three of aniseseed, two each of sweetshrub, Franklin tree, sweet gum, birch, and beech, in addition to two- four- and eight-ounce packets of single types of many more. He asked for twenty ounces of rhododendron seeds, and the acorns of all kinds of oaks. Lelieur enjoined du Pont to gather all of these himself, a most unreasonable demand to make of a man working long hours, beset by delays and difficulties in building and putting his powder factory into operation. Possibly du Pont did find time to gather some in person, but he also had the assistance of Kin at the Charleston garden and Saulnier at Hackensack.

The exchange between Lelieur and du Pont was carried on for a number of years. One shipment from the Brandywine consisted of five barrels of white oak acorns, "enough," said Irénée, "to plant a forest," a new pear tree recently developed, and some pecan trees unknown in France. Lelieur was kept informed of newly discovered species and received seeds or cuttings of them. In return Irénée asked for a certain kind of grape, 'White Corinth,' a seedless variety which was something of a rarity in America. The brig *Swift* that departed Bordeaux for the United States on February 20, 1804, carried three cases of garden plants and trees weighing three quarters of a ton consigned by Lelieur to du Pont, who received them in April, not too late for spring planting. The following March he shared the shipment with his friend Preudhomme at Bergen Point, sending him a box containing thirty-six varieties of grafts.

In 1806 Irénée wrote a letter to Lelieur introducing to him Jean-Baptiste Theodore Leschenault, a naturalist newly arrived in the United States from the East Indies with "very beautiful collections of every kind in both botany and natural history." Leschenault was entertained at Eleutherian Mills before returning to France, a welcome opportunity for Irénée to discuss his favorite subject with a professional botanist. Leschenault, du Pont informed Lelieur, would be able to tell him about "the 'children' you sent me, of which I have taken the greatest care and which are growing finely. Many of them already have fruit." It pleased du Pont to know that Leschenault was going to turn over to the French government his valuable and exotic collections—collections that could become a source of national wealth. A genus of Australian plants that have the bluest flowers known to exist in nature has been given Leschenault's name.

Visitors to the du Pont home (fig. 16) often departed taking with them gifts of seeds, nuts, and cuttings for planting in their own gardens, a practice by which those of European origin became more

Fig. 16 Front view of the residence at Eleutherian Mills, sketched by Eleuthera du Pont about 1823.

widely distributed in this country. Peter Regnier, a house guest from Louisiana in 1806, wrote in his bread-and-butter note, "Pray give my regards to Madame du Pont and tell her that the nuts and seeds she gave me went to Louisiana with my gardener; that I hope everything will be planted within a month and that I shall be there in time to eat some of her excellent melons."

Business callers arrived on horseback or in a carriage, traversing the road that divided the garden and orchard on one side from the barn area on the other. Du Pont's office was in his home, and there is little doubt that flowers, fruit trees, crops, and animals intruded into many a conversation that had begun with talk about the powder business. The office looked out upon a piazza brightened with a medley of colorful potted plants (plate 5). Some of these were the gifts of neighbors, relatives, and visitors from a distance who were aware of Irénée's and Sophie's fondness for flowers. When young men began calling upon du Pont's marriageable daughters, Victorine, Evelina, Eleuthera, and Sophie, the more perceptive swains knew the tokens of affection that were most welcome. Long before this, when the sons and daughters were quite young, they had been encouraged to make individual gardens of their own; to collect, sketch, and press leaves and flowers; to gather shells; to keep a small menagerie of household and barnyard pets; and to make stone and mineral collections.

The letters that passed between the young people of the family when away at school and the folks at home often mentioned their

Fig. 17 Sketch of Eleutherian Mills by the Baroness Hyde de Neuville, 1817, showing the du Pont home overlooking the powder mill refinery.

natural history collections, how the pets were faring, and what was blooming in their gardens. Typical was this note from Victorine to her sister Evelina at school in Philadelphia, "The lilacs are all in bloom as well as the lilies of the valley. Your white daffodils have also unfolded their snowy leaves and spread the most delicious fragrance throughout the garden." She informed brother Alfred that all was well with his garden, "but it would be better if you were here to take care of it." Ten-year-old Henry du Pont, the second son, was a very homesick boy attending an academy in Germantown in 1822. He was cheered up by letters from his older sisters filled with chitchat: Alfred, the older brother, was getting some new minerals for Henry's collection; a crocodile and a toad had been preserved in turpentine; Sophie, twelve years old, had made a moss garden; the fuschias, jessamines, and chrysanthemums were blooming; a rose bush Eleuthera had grown had nineteen roses, all blooming at one time; but all the butterflies had disappeared.

Henry wrote home telling of his plans to make imitations of the floating gardens of Mexico when he next came home on vacation. He had a garden at school in 1824, so news of its progress was relayed to the family in May and June when the hyacinths were fading but the pinks, sweet williams, mock oranges, and roses were in bloom. His enthusiasm shows in this line to Sophie: "You cannot think how beautiful my garden looks. I have a great many roses." The next year he helped form a philosophical society at school and was elected its president. Henry thought up the society's motto— "Ignorance is the sting of the human heart"—and promoted a project of making a collection of butterflies and collecting and drying flowers for preservation.

Letters from his sisters and brothers when he became a cadet at the United States Military Academy at West Point in 1829 show a continuing awareness and love of nature. Eleuthera described for him a late spring walk along the Brandywine after a visit to their friends the Gilpins, who lived downstream:

We came home all along the creek to see some beautiful Fringe trees which Papa had told us were in bloom near Rockford. We found them perfectly white with flowers & were very sorry that as they were on the other side of the creek we could not reach them. . . .

I have been drawing some flowers from nature lately. I like doing this very much and wish I could draw nothing else.

Plate 5 View from the rear piazza of Eleutherian Mills. Photograph by Lautman.

Plate 6 Brandywine Woods. Photograph by Lautman.

After graduating from the academy and serving a year in the army on the Alabama frontier, Henry came home to work in the powder mills. He was one of the vice-presidents of the reorganized Agricultural Society of New Castle County founded in 1836. His interest in minerals led him to write a lengthy memoir on the mineralogy of Delaware. Henry and his bride, Louisa Gerhard of Philadelphia, became master and mistress of Eleutherian Mills in 1837, three years after the death of his father, and over the next fifty years they enlarged and developed it as a flourishing estate and farming property.

Fig. 18 François André Michaux. Courtesy of Royal Botanic Gardens, Kew, England.

CHAPTER V

Botanizing in Brandywine Woods

I was so busy last summer that I have hardly been able to collect
anything at all. Now, however, I have settled down at last. I have
bought property situated on Brandywine Creek near Wilmington, state
of Delaware. . . . Any leisure I may have will be dedicated to natural
history research, which in this country has the double attraction of
the variety of the objects as well as their novelty.

E. I. du Pont to Alexandre Brongniart, 1802

A NUMBER of European naturalists on prolonged visits to this
country in the early 1800s were guests of Irénée du Pont at his
Brandywine home. Some he first met in Philadelphia, to which he
made frequent business trips and where a number of his friends and
business associates were men also interested in the natural sciences.
John Vaughan, merchant and powder agent, and the energetic secretary of the American Philosophical Society, was one who shared
Irénée's enthusiasm for botany. Irénée was elected to membership in
the society in 1807. Through Vaughan he made the acquaintance of
Constantine S. Rafinesque, a young naturalist most recently from
Marseilles who was entertained at Eleutherian Mills in the fall of
1804. Rafinesque enjoyed his stay, doing some botanizing in the
Brandywine woods (plate 6), acquiring some new plants to take
away with him, and discussing with Irénée such esoteric subjects as
the classification of hickory nuts. He learned enough about Delaware
flora to write an account entitled "Florula Delawarica," a catalogue
that was tentatively accepted for publication in the *Philadelphia Med-
ical and Physical Journal* but which never appeared in print.

There were local mushrooms of a type unknown to Rafinesque
that he asked Charles Dalmas to sketch for him. He was making a
collection of American plants, more of which he hoped to acquire
on a second visit to Delaware, where he believed at least a hundred
of them grew. When he left the Brandywine for Philadelphia, he
took along one of Irénée's prized new books, André Michaux's *Flora*

Boreali-Americana. Rafinesque had to return to Sicily before he could make a return visit, but when the ship on which he sailed down the Delaware had to anchor off New Castle he penned a gracious note to Irénée, telling him he had left the borrowed book with Vaughan and expressing his appreciation for the hospitality du Pont had extended to him: "I remember the many courtesies with which you have overwhelmed me in our short acquaintance. I can only repeat to you my assurance of the memory I shall always keep of your kindness to me. I hope to send you a little collection of seeds from Sicily if you would care for it."

With François André Michaux (fig. 18), a friendship developed that erased whatever ill will Irénée may initially have had toward him as the "destroyer" of the French gardens in America. It began with correspondence pertaining to Kin's and Saulnier's garden accounts, the selection and shipping of items from their gardens to France, and the final disposition of the two nurseries. Michaux enjoyed du Pont's hospitality on several occasions, walking with him through the neighboring woods and studying the splendid trees to be found there. Michaux was gathering material for a book he was writing on American trees, and in this he enlisted du Pont's collaboration. Responding, Irénée collected and sent to him forty boxes of acorns and seeds (fig. 19), twenty-nine of which were filled with the acorns of ten species of oaks; ten boxes of seeds of the butternut, shellbark, pignut, mockernut, beechnut, sassafras, chinquapin, tupelo, wild cherry, chestnut, black birch, white, red, and black ash, and sweet gum. In the fortieth box were dogwood, roots of "grape leaves," shoots of the Spitzemberg apple to be grafted, and cuttings of other good apple stocks.

Twelve of the twenty-nine boxes of acorns were filled with black oak acorns, a tree highly regarded by Michaux both for its appearance and for special qualities that gave it many valuable uses. His acknowledgment of the assistance given him in propagating black oaks in France is implied in this statement written some years after Irénée had made his shipment: "This is why, during my visit to North America, I decided to send back to France many seeds of this species. There are now in the nurseries of the imperial bureau of forests and waters more than twenty thousand young plants whose vigorous growth assures their propagation in the imperial forests."

Michaux returned to France in 1808, taking with him letters and

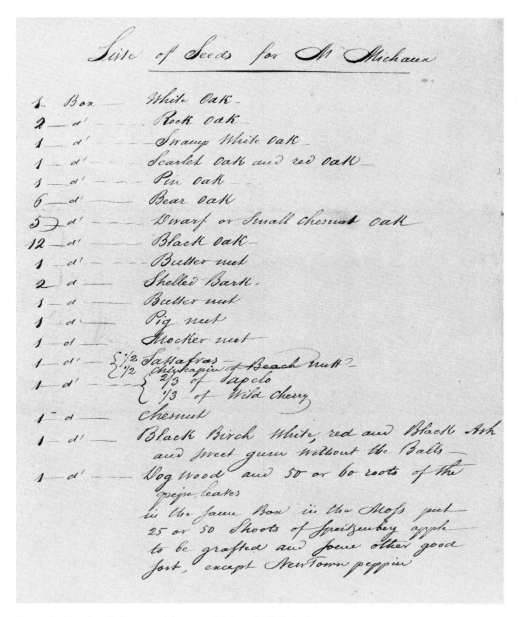

Fig. 19 Packing list of plant materials sent to Michaux by E. I. du Pont.

packages from Irénée and Victor to be given to their father. Among the missives was a sketch of the powder mills which showed the du Pont home visible in a patch of woods on the bluff overlooking the factory. Drawn by Dalmas, Mrs. du Pont's brother, the sketch was to be shown to the French shareholders as a supplemental item to Irénée's annual report. By the original agreement that created the business, the shareholders were to vote in 1809 whether to continue the powder venture or to liquidate it.

Michaux's monumental work on American trees, *Histoire des arbres forestiers de l'Amérique septentrionale,* was prepared for publication in both France and the United States. The title of the English-language edition was *The North American Sylva,* first published in 1817, and it went through three editions by 1857. For the American edition Michaux consulted Irénée in 1810 about the scope of the subject, illustrations to be used, and costs and distribution. He instructed his Philadelphia publishers, Bradford and Inskeep, to send all copy to du Pont for examination and correction before it was printed. Michaux and du Pont, with Vaughan of the American Philosophical Society, had discussed the undertaking years earlier, when Michaux had been du Pont's guest, and had been encouraged by him to write the book. It is apparent that, though du Pont was not a professional botanist, men of that profession regarded him as far more than a dilettante and respected his knowledge and counsel.

Michaux carried on his "naturalizing" of American plants and trees at his home at Vauréal on the Oise (plate 4) and at an estate he administered at Harcourt near Bernay. When he died in 1855 his tomb was placed in a grove at Vauréal amid plants and trees that had been brought from America. Who can say but that some of these had come from the richly wooded areas along the Brandywine surrounding du Pont's home?

Recognition of the contributions of the Michaux, father and son, to forestry research and tree propagation was made a little less than a century later, in 1953, when a memorial, the Quercetum Michaux, was established at the Morris Arboretum near Philadelphia. It is a collection of oak trees assembled from all parts of the world, available for study by botanists and horticulturists. It was made possible in part by a legacy left by the younger Michaux to the American Philosophical Society in appreciation of the hospitality and assistance that had been extended to his father and to himself during their sojourns in the United States.

A fairly frequent visitor to Eleutherian Mills before he returned to his native Portugal in 1820 was the eminent Abbé Corréa da Serra (1750–1823), Portuguese minister plenipotentiary, a man of science with a special interest in botany, whom du Pont had come to know through associations in the American Philosophical Society. On his last visit before departing for home, the Abbé was taken on a tour of the family garden by Victorine. They paused longest in one of the arbors to examine some tall greenish-yellow flowers which the du Pont children had named "Mr. Corréa," a species of *Menispermum,* or moonseed, the seeds of which the Abbé had given their father some years earlier.

Two illustrator-naturalists who spent some time in the Brandywine region during the 1820s were Auguste Plée (1787–1825), and Charles Alexandre Lesueur (1778–1857). Plée spent part of the summer of 1821 convalescing from illness at the summer home of M. Mathieu de Lesseps, French consul in Philadelphia and father of the engineer of the Suez Canal. Lesueur, who was later to become director of the museum at Le Havre, was du Pont's guest in 1822. Both visitors did sketches of a number of local scenes, gardens, homes, and woodlands in the vicinity of the stream.

Du Pont tried his hand at writing on botanical subjects in a very modest way. Among his papers is a lengthy illustrated memoir on an abundant sea plant that he called "Raisin de mer," or "Raisin du tropique," presumably sea grape, *Coccolobis uvifera,* found on the shores of the Gulf of Mexico. For Dr. James Mease of Philadelphia, editor of the *Archives of Useful Knowledge,* a journal designed to stimulate and improve agriculture, the arts, and manufactures, he wrote an essay on the cultivation and uses of millet, a fine grain cereal. He presented it to Mease in 1808, submitting his small contribution in botanical idiom: "I will, with great pleasure, offer you my *grain of millet* if acceptable," and signing himself "A Delaware Farmer." A search of the *Archives* for the three years it was published, 1809–1811, failed to locate the article; so presumably the "Delaware Farmer" received a rejection slip.

Mease tapped du Pont's store of practical knowledge on the uses of plants on another occasion when he inquired how "green soap" was colored. Hempseed oil, du Pont replied, was the best coloring agent, but it was scarce and costly in this country, so American soap manufacturers used such substitutes as rapeseed oil, combined a little indigo with it, and got a nice green-colored soap. If they used linseed or poppy oil, they added curcuma and indigo to produce the green color.

His knowledge of trees and woods was put to practical use in making the charcoal that went into the composition of black powder. Powder makers had found that black willow produced the best charcoal, but du Pont carried on experiments with various other woods. He had reason to believe that an exotic from China, arborescent hemp, would make a fine inflammable charcoal. It was not available in this country but he knew it grew in the Jardin des Plantes in Paris, so he requested his father to obtain some seeds from his former "school" and send them to him.

Knowledge of the qualities of different types of woods used in construction served him well when building his mills. It was the fine stand of trees on the land he bought in 1802 for his factory that made it a good buy; in cutting his own timber, he estimated he could save about one third of his building costs. Water-wheel shafts and buckets were made of durable white oak, and gudgeons were hewn from lignum vitae or such Cuban hardwoods as *acuna, cabrahache* (ironwood), or *bois éternel* (eternal wood). And the right kinds of wood had to be chosen for the planking of dams and for the mortars and pestles of his stamping mills.

Live trees bearing fruits or nuts, flowers, flowering shrubs, and scented herbs pleased the aesthete in du Pont, but they also satisfied the strong practical bent of his character. To him the many faces of nature were beautiful and evocative, enriching the spirit and gladdening the eye, but nature was also the provider of many things man needed for maintaining life, adding to his well-being and comfort, and supplying the raw materials for much of his economic "busyness."

CHAPTER VI

The Gardens at Eleutherian Mills

The great charm of this garden, like all those that the hand of time
has touched, was its luxuriance, and the reminder everywhere that age
alone could produce its wonderful effect.

From "A Lost Garden" by Mrs. Antoine L.
(Victorine E. du Pont) Foster

IRÉNÉE'S success in the powder business was hard earned.
Though he had the assistance of his brother-in-law Charles
Dalmas during the early years, and of his son Alfred Victor when
Alfred became twenty years of age in 1818, it was in fact a one-man
enterprise with all the responsibility falling upon him and a mul-
tiplicity of details to keep an eye on. More land was bought or
leased for the erection of new mills, for growing field crops, for
enlarging the orchard, and for the grazing and pasturing of sheep,
cattle, and horses. Du Pont kept a large flock of Merino sheep,
breeding finer strains from his prize full-blooded rams, Don Pedro
and Sanchez. The fleeces from his flock produced an excellent wool
that was made into fine cloth at the Louviers Woolen Mill directed
by his brother Victor, across the Brandywine from the powder mills.
Improving the bloodlines of horses was another feature of his animal
husbandry, attested to by the breeding records, correspondence, and
periodic inventories of all the livestock. He became a member of the
Philadelphia Society for Promoting Agriculture in 1808 and ten
years later joined the New Castle County Agricultural Society.

The hub of the farming activity was the large barn (fig. 20) with
stables and wagon sheds on the north side of the road that led directly to the house. On the south side of this road was the family
garden, originally a little over an acre in extent but by the mid-1820s
doubled in size. Here, in parterres bordered by dwarf and espaliered
peach and pear trees, grew flowers, herbs, and vegetables. For many
years the routine tending of the garden was done by John Prevost,
and after him by Bernard Reilly. Prevost is one of the few persons not

of the family to be buried in the du Pont cemetery in Sand Hole Woods which overlooks the garden long in his care. For the kitchen were grown beets, carrots, turnips and parsnips, cabbage, broccoli, peas, beans, rhubarb, and onions. There were gooseberry, raspberry, and currant bushes, beds of strawberries, and patches of melons. A variety of seasonings was provided by such herbs as garlic, caraway, sweet marjoram, sweet basil, salsify, and summer savory. The garden

Fig. 20 The barn at Eleutherian Mills, late nineteenth century.

was a flower lover's delight, offering a colorful array of annuals, perennials, ornamental plants, and shrubs that perfumed the air with mingled scents—roses, irises, lilies of the valley, columbines, camellias, mignonettes, nasturtiums, sweet peas, chrysanthemums, jessamines, fuschias, altheas, laburnums, lilacs, spireas, japonicas, hydrangeas, snowberries, hawthorns, lady apples, and magnolias. Wildflowers in the nearby woods that caught their fancy were dug

up by the children and transplanted into the garden to be natural-
ized. Victorine wrote of finding some scarlet columbines among
hillside rocks to a younger sister in 1822: "I thought them so pretty
that I brought home many with the roots, and planted them in our
garden."

Bordering the garden at the far end was a long grape arbor that
extended two thirds of the way across its width; the other third
consisted of trellises and fencing on which both grape and hop vines
grew. Du Pont continued the custom of the vintage, making wine
in early fall from the 'Chasselas,' 'Muscat Blanc,' 'Muscat violet,'
'Corinth,' and 'Précox' grapes that he grew. From the cherry trees
growing on the north side of the garden and in the orchard he made
a favorite family drink, cherry bounce. In later years boxwood borders, broken here and there by a pink or white hawthorn, a yew, or a
tree hydrangea, replaced the espaliered fruit trees that had enclosed
some of the beds. Evelina du Pont, the eldest daughter of Henry and
Louisa du Pont, who was born at Eleutherian Mills in 1840, recalled
when in her nineties that gardens patterned after French gardens had
paths of yellow gravel that were bordered with red bricks (fig. 21).
Flowers were planted close to the brick borders and vegetables were
planted in the center of the beds. A practical, observant lady, she
also opined that mint should always be planted on the western side
of the garden because it spread westward as it grew; planted elsewhere it would soon intrude upon other plantings.

A younger sister of Evelina's, Victorine Elizabeth (Mrs. Antoine L.
Foster, 1849–1934), looking back upon her childhood at Eleutherian
Mills, had these cherished memories of the family garden, which to
her, writing in the 1920s, had become "A Lost Garden":

The lovely old garden where three generations of happy children played,
laid out early in the last century, was rather an unusual one with its rare
trees and plants.

At the corner of the roads, facing the house, the entrance through a gate
up five steps to the top of the circular retaining wall was quaint and
effective. At right angles to the path which led to the center of the
garden was a hedge of white and purple lilacs carpeted with lilies-of-the-
valley and periwinkle. Along the paths were large box-bordered beds
with high round box bushes at each corner. The flower borders were
planted with flowers, shrubs, and occasionally small trees. Vegetables and
small fruit filled the center of the beds, and a small formal garden was

Fig. 21 The du Pont garden as it appeared in 1873 when sketched by Theophilus P. Chandler, son-in-law of Henry du Pont.

70

filled with hyacinths and tulips early in the season and later with annuals and autumnal crocuses. At the garden pump on an ivy-covered
wall and broad platform we loved to sit and on warm summer evenings
it was our delight to water favorite flowers from the large round hogshead
full of water.

In the box borders in the spring nothing could be more lovely than the
two large hawthorne trees, pink and white, like big nosegays, the *Pyrus
japonicas,* wisterias, the lilac hedge in full bloom and two double-flower-
ing apple trees spreading over an attractive arbor.

Against the picket fence on the north side of the garden ran a lovely
rose border of yellow Harrisoni and little pink and white Burnett roses,
the earliest of all to bloom, and with the June roses came a very beautiful
French single rose, a dark crimson with a yellow center which was re-
puted to possess medicinal value and was much prized in the garden. A
large tree of sweet-scented magnolia (*Magnolia glauca*) covered with
white blossoms was also growing there and commanded attention.

The beds of ripe French strawberries (the wild strawberry of France)
with its delicious perfume and flavor, cherries red and white and the big
strawberries made the garden a paradise for fruit lovers, the September
days bringing pears and grapes, chestnuts and autumn flowers.

On the broad walk at the top of the garden with grape-covered trellises
on one side and a border of four o'clocks on the other we loved to
walk and watch the Humming Birds and Night Moths dart in and out
of the bright-colored flowers. Nearby was the well-assorted herb bed with
the bright blossoms of Tansy, yellow being the dominant tone.

The great charm of this garden, like all those that the hand of time has
touched, was its luxuriance, and the reminder everywhere that age alone
could produce its wonderful effect.

From the rare seeds sent from the Jardin des Plantes in Paris was the
Papaver orientale (the first in America) and people came often to see these
flowers in bloom.

To keep it fresh in her mind, Mrs. Foster sketched a plan of the
garden as she recalled its appearance about 1880, when the garden
was over seventy-five years old (fig. 22). Its formal, geometric design
was a counterpart of the classical style gardens of eighteenth century
France. There was a bed of roses for cutting and also a formal rose
garden laid out *en parterre* with paths radiating to the four corners
from a center circle of bushes. Some of the roses were those that had

71

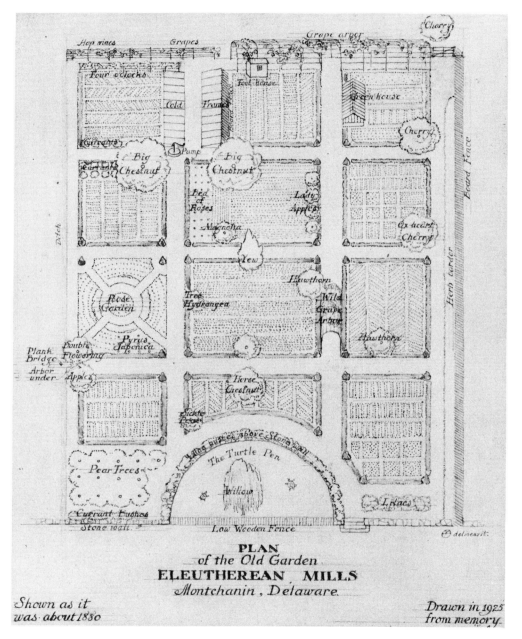

Fig. 22 Design of the du Pont garden drawn by Mrs. Victorine E. (du Pont) Foster.

been sent by Lelieur: 'Rose à cent feuilles,' 'Rose des quatre saisons,' 'Rose pompone,' and 'Rose ponceau.' From a New York nursery, du Pont added 'Napoleon,' 'Perpetuelle,' 'Grand Monarque,' 'Jaune Double,' 'Impératrice Josephine,' 'Monsieur Rouge,' 'Monsieur Blanc,' 'Couleur de Bronze,' 'Marie Louise,' 'Sultane favorite,' and 'Rose du Roi.' Thousands of new varieties have since been developed by rosarians, but nurseries specializing in old-fashioned roses can still supply a few of those found in the first du Pont garden, 'Empress Josephine' and 'Rose du Roi' being two that appear in some catalogues.

Parts of the garden were shaded by large chestnut trees which, according to family tradition, were the first French chestnut trees grown in the United States. A pink horse chestnut, or buckeye, growing on the lawn between the house and the garden (plate 7) was studied by Charles S. Sargent, director of the Arnold Arboretum in 1923. He identified it as a hybrid of *Aesculus neglecta* and *Aesculus pavia* and gave it the name *Aesculus (X) dupontii* because of the very strong supposition that it had been introduced by Irénée du Pont. In the *Journal of the Arnold Arboretum* for 1924 Sargent described it as an unusual and attractive tree, and acknowledged the sustained interest of the du Pont family in horticulture throughout four generations. Whether it had been affixed to this tree or to another buckeye on the property is not known, but a brass plate bearing this legend has recently been found on the grounds:

BUCKEYE TREE

GROWN FROM NUT PROCURED IN GEORGIA

WHILE RETURNING FROM A BUSINESS TRIP

TO NEW ORLEANS ON HORSE BACK

BY

E. I. DU PONT IN 1817

Nut gathering began with the blowing of the "chestnut wind" in the crisp days of early October.

Du Pont's friends and business callers admired his trees and often asked for seeds, grafts, or cuttings. A typical request was this one from Bernard M'Mahon of Philadelphia, nurseryman and author of gardening books:

I take the liberty of soliciting from you a few scions or grafts of any particular kinds of pears, apples, plums, or cherries which have borne fruit with you, and which you esteem and consider deserving of cultivation. My object is not a numerous variety, but a selection of the best kinds for the different seasons of the year. Could you oblige me with these, and a few succors [sic] or plants of the pompon rose, or any other roses that you esteem, you would confer a great favor on me, and I would return the compliment in any way in my power. I am very desirous of obtaining a plant or even a few grafts of the large French Chestnut (Marron de Lyons) which you probably can accommodate me with.

The cold winter of 1819–1820 killed off many trees and plants in the Delaware area. James Rogers of New Castle lost all the raspberry bushes which du Pont had given him the previous spring. In March 1820 he asked Irénée for some replacements—"a repetition of your liberality"— if he could spare them.

Henry M. Ridgely of Dover, du Pont's attorney, was sent a box of fruit grafts—pears, apples, and cherries, each identified by its French name and the number it bore in du Pont's orchard, and a pot containing Spanish chestnuts that were beginning to sprout. Irénée instructed Ridgely to upset the pot carefully to get them out without breaking the buds and then plant each one in a separate pot and sink them in the ground of his garden. From Ridgely he in turn asked for scions of a particular dwarf apple tree growing on the Ridgely farm. The stocks of this tree were especially good to graft other apples on, and it was a very pretty tree when in bloom. Ridgely offered him some scions of the 'Summer Grixon' and the 'Cane Apple,' fine fall and early winter apples he had never seen growing elsewhere in New Castle County. In a sheltered place in his garden, Irénée planted an orange tree given to him by one of the Philadelphia coopers who made kegs for the powder factory.

In the upper part of the garden were cold frames, a tool shed, a greenhouse, and a pump from which a hogshead nearby was kept filled with water. Daughter Victorine, a young widow who lived with her parents, made the greenhouse her special domain, spending many hours there. The flowers grown in the greenhouse were spoken of as "Vic's flowers" by other members of the family. When a second greenhouse was erected closer to the dwelling, she was very happy because it was larger, and, being nearer to the house, she could work in it every day, even in bad weather. When she had particular success she could not resist a little boasting: "I wish you could see the

Plate 7 Blossom of hybrid horsechestnut tree. Photograph by Herzog.

Plate 8 Watercolor of lily by Sophie du Pont.

chrysanthemums, they never were so handsome. I also have a camelia Japonica in bloom, larger than any I ever saw."

The fertility of du Pont's garden, abetted by the green thumb of the gardener, produced a giant sunflower in the summer of 1823 that measured forty inches in circumference and thirteen inches in diameter. Delighted with it, Victorine reported: "This wonderful Sunflower may be seen at the house of the cultivator, where persons desirous of procuring seed must apply. We rejoice in the superior fertility of the Tancopanican [the Indian name for Brandywine], as this Sunflower was more than 10 inches larger than one which was mentioned in a late gazette under the title of Mammoth."

A place such as Bartram's Gardens, the oldest and best-known nursery in America, located at the southern extremity of Philadelphia, was a magnet to Irénée on his routine trips to the city. At one time, contemplating some new plantings of ornamentals, he purchased from the Bartram nursery some variegated camellias, double altheas, snowberries, honeysuckles, laburnums, Franklinias, and Champney roses. He wanted some pink spirea, but was informed it was too early in the season to take it from the ground, and that the English name for spirea was meadowsweet. We do not know if Irénée was then aware of the existence of Peirce's Park, an arboretum near Kennett Square, Pennsylvania, about ten miles from his home, which a century later was to become the world-famed Longwood Gardens, created by one of his own great-grandsons.

Powder agents in more distant places supplied du Pont with specimens that did not grow in Delaware. He asked his Pittsburgh representative, Boggs and Wrenshall, to send him a bushel of seeds of the honey locust tree. This odd tree, native to the woods of western Pennsylvania, sprouted clusters of thorns directly from its main trunk. Du Pont knew that the agents were too busy to handle this chore personally, but he suggested that they speak to some farmers in their neighborhood and have the farmers' children gather up the large pods and take out the seeds, which resembled small beans. The request was fulfilled, as is evident in the number of honey locust trees to be found growing at Eleutherian Mills and in the powder yards nearby. At another time a New York supplier of black lead, used in glazing powder, sent a New Year's gift of two cases and a barrel of newly imported "Dutch Flower Roots"—hyacinths, tulips, and narcissuses—for planting in the family garden.

The demands of his expanding business, the time needed for his growing family and for community activities, and the War of 1812–1815 forced du Pont to curtail shipping botanical items to France. But requests continued to come intermittently from friends and correspondents. Some friends in France wanted to try growing American tobacco, so at Irénée's request his agent in Richmond, Virginia, Gallego, Richards and Company, procured four quarts of the best seed available from the last crop, which he sent to France in time for the tobacco planting season.

How common a practice it was is not clear, but du Pont sometimes culled his gardens and orchard for items to send to agents in the midwestern cities. Henry Von Phul of St. Louis, when in the East making arrangements to handle Du Pont powder, visited the mills and was a guest of the family. He was taken on a stroll through the garden and orchard and admired much that he saw. Not long after this, du Pont sent Von Phul a box containing lady apples, French chestnuts, variegated and pale-colored roses, crocuses, double Parma and double common violets, raspberries, and red and white French strawberries for planting in his garden in St. Louis, then a raw, rough frontier town. All arrived in good time for planting. Powder to pacify and plants to beautify made an interesting juxtaposition of civilizing forces in the taming of the American West.

Though he had a gardener and helpers who could do the chores, du Pont found that digging, planting, tending, pruning, and picking in the garden and orchard were good exercise and a welcome escape when business cares bore oppressively upon him. While he was recuperating from an accident that limited his activities and kept him confined for a month, his friend John Vaughan in Philadelphia inquired about the state of his health. He received this reply: "Our E. I. du Pont has the pleasure to inform you that he is now out of pain; he is well now but only weak. Our wounded man was digging his garden at 6 o'clock the next morning."

We can only conjecture whether Irénée planted according to its instructions, but laid in between pages of *The Practical Farmer: Being a New and Compendious System of Husbandry,* a book by John Spurrier published in Wilmington in 1793, were these

Rules for Planting Trees

In the first place, dig a hole three feet and a half square, and 21 inches deep, (four weeks before you plant, which must be done three or four days after new moon) take some new earth out of the woods, and fill the hole about nine inches—take four quarts of oats for every tree you wish to plant—set your tree in, and scatter about a quart and a pint about the roots, then a larger quantity of new earth, and so on alternately till the hole is filled up. In the place of the oats you may use the shavings of three horns with similar effect.

This enforced respite at home allowed Irénée more time for reading and browsing among his books. The family library numbered about four thousand volumes and reflected his own catholicity of interests and those of his father, from whom he had inherited much of the collection. Botany, horticulture, agriculture, and natural history were subjects represented by a hundred titles, most of them French publications, a number in multivolume editions. On the shelves of the library were these recognized classics:

Abrégé du système de la nature. Carl von Linné
Catalogue alphabétique des arbres et arbrisseaux, qui croissent naturelle-
    ment dans les Etats-Unis. Humphry Marshall
Dictionnaire élémentaire de botanique. Pierre Bulliard
Histoire naturelle. Georges Louis L. de Buffon
Instruction pour les jardins fruitiers et potagers. Jean de La Quintinie
Manuel de botanique. François Lebreton
Mémoires de physique et d'histoire naturelle. Jean Baptiste P. A. Lamarck
Principes de botanique. Étienne Pierre Ventenat

There were books on forestry and forest conservation and management, on land cultivation and farming methods, on entomology and zoology, on rural architecture, and economic studies that discussed the relationship of agriculture to commerce, industry, and the arts. Du Pont subscribed to the *American Farmer*, the *Farmer and Gardener*, the *Cabinet of Natural History*, and the *Emporium of all the Arts and Sciences*. He received the memoirs, journals, and proceedings of a number of French, English, and American agricultural, scientific, and philosophical societies. On the shelves of the family library there was no dearth of reading material in their favorite subjects for Irénée and his sons and daughters.

CHAPTER VII

Gardeners of the Second Generation

Our parents were both very fond of flowers, and we inherited the taste.

Eleuthera du Pont Smith to Lilia Bienaymé, 1853

OF DU PONT'S seven children, the eldest, Victorine, was her father's most devoted disciple in the subject of botany. When he was away on business trips he made it a practice to observe the local flora and to keep his eyes open for new and unusual specimens to acquire for her collections. From Providence, Rhode Island, in mid-July 1821, after he had returned from a ride in the countryside, he wrote to her:

I found the native barberry growing wild and in great abundance all along the roads. The season is more than three weeks beyond ours; the elders are beginning to bloom, the grains are green and the cherries are still on the trees. As I did not have you with me to examine plants and as I could not take back to you the new kinds that I found, I spent the evening gathering minerals for Alfred, which is not difficult here, where the bones of the earth are very near the skin.

Surviving among family papers is an herbarium, a collection of pressed and mounted specimens of plants and flowers, 233 in number, all labeled and classified. No signature appears to tell who put it together, but the handwriting suggests it was Victorine's work. A copybook of hers contains drawings of stems and leaves and has identifying captions taken from Drummond's *First Steps to Botany*. Other positive evidence of her serious interest are two manuals which she compiled in 1837 (fig. 23). In these are found notes on genera, orders, and classes of many plants and flowers, the characteristics of each that help to identify it, the best habitat for growth, and ways to judge the health of plants and flowers. Scattered through the pages are precise, carefully drawn sketches of leaves, flowers, stems, and buds. The cover of one manual shows a vernal scene beneath which appears a verse phrased in the romantic style of the day:

> Come, gentle Spring! etherial Mildness! come;
> And from the bosom of your dropping cloud,
> While music makes around, veil'd in a shower
> Of shadowing roses, on our plains descend.

After her mother's death in 1828, Victorine became her father's hostess, receiving business callers and entertaining guests and relatives visiting Eleutherian Mills. Invariably, if the weather was pleasant and the visitors showed the slightest interest, they were taken on a walk through the garden and into the orchard and bordering woods. One young friend complained she was more tired after an extensive tour with Victorine than she was walking the four miles from Wilmington. Between 1830 and 1834 Victorine and her unmarried sisters still living at home kept an intimate family diary called "The Tancopanican Chronicle" in which they entered notes about their visitors and jotted down personal comments about some of them. During those five years the daughters calculated that they had entertained 877 guests, many of whom had brought plants, shrubs, seeds, and flowers as gifts to their hostesses and their father.

Victorine's younger sisters, Eleuthera and Sophie, were collectors who pressed flowers, leaves, and ferns and mounted them in pocket-size binders (fig. 24). They were not as careful and consistent as Victorine in their identifications, but usually the place and date where a particular specimen was found were written adjacent to it. These few entries suggest they collected wherever opportunity allowed:

"The Moss Grotto," West Point, September 7, 1829
Bartram's Garden, Philadelphia, May 4, 1830
Hagley, Monday night, July 5, 1830
Impatiens, from Mr. Jefferson's Hortus siccus, Monticello, May 21, 1831

The item plucked at Bartram's was a pink, and from the grounds at Hagley they had picked and mounted two tiny roses that caught their fancy.

During the 1840s and 1850s the du Pont women journeyed abroad several times, a part of their itineraries taken up with botanizing trips in the British Isles, France, Spain, Portugal, and Minorca. Enclosed with their letters were packets of seeds. The specimens they

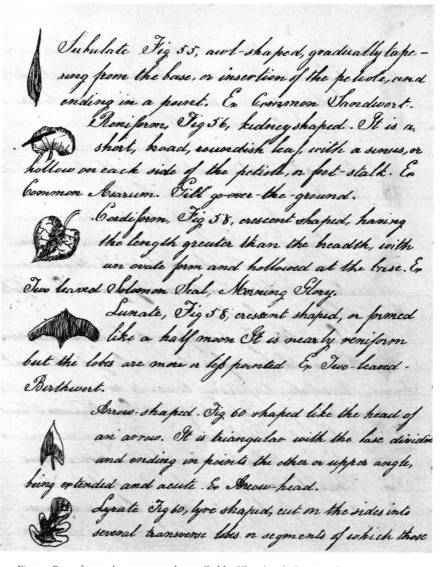

Subulate Fig 55, awl-shaped, gradually tapering from the base, or insertion of the petiole, and ending in a point. Ex Common Sandwort.

Reniform, Fig 56, kidney shaped. It is a short, broad, roundish leaf, with a sinus, or hollow on each side of the petiole, or foot-stalk. Ex Common Asarum. Gill go-over-the-ground.

Cordiform, Fig 58, crescent shaped, having the length greater than the breadth, with an ovate form and hollowed at the base. Ex Two leaved Solomon Seal, Morning Glory.

Lunate, Fig 58, crescent shaped, or formed like a half moon It is nearly reniform but the lobes are more or less pointed Ex Two-leaved-Birthwort.

Arrow-shaped. Fig 60 shaped like the head of an arrow. It is triangular with the base divided and ending in points the other or upper angle, being extended and acute. Ex Arrow-head.

Lyrate Fig 60, lyre shaped, cut on the sides into several transverse lobes or segments of which those

Fig. 23 Pages from a botany manual compiled by Victorine du Pont in 1837.

nearest the stem are the smallest Ex Lyre leaved Sage.

Panduriform, Fig 61 fiddle-shaped. It is long, broad at the two extremities, and narrow in the middle. Ex Virginia Bindweed.

Runcinate, Fig 62 lion-toothed cut into many transverse, acute segments pointing backwards. Ex Dandelion.

Hastate, Fig 63, halbert-shaped. The shape is triangular, the base spreading, and ending in two opposite angles the form oblong terminating in a point with the sides a little hollowed. Ex Bittersweed, Canary Sage.

Sinuate, Fig. 64, cut into rounded lobes, or wide opening the margins bending in and out Ex Water Hore hound, Red Oak.

Pinnatifid, Fig 65, wingcleft. It is transversely wing divided into small lobes, or oblong segments, but not reaching to the midrib Ex Crow Foot Canary Bill. Wild Peppergrass.

Laciniate, Fig 66 jagged, cut into numerous, irregu lar portions, or lobes, which are again subdivided,

Fig. 24 Herbarium specimen picked by Sophie du Pont in 1826 from Washington's tomb at Mount Vernon.

brought home were mounted and copied in water colors in their sketchbooks (plate 8). These are good renderings, for as students at Madame Rivardi's school in Philadelphia the girls had received instruction in art which developed a latent natural talent, possibly derived from the maternal side of the family.

There is a family story about their cousin Charles I. du Pont (1797–1869) that the women must have chuckled over. When he visited Paris he was much impressed by the splendid horse-chestnut trees growing in the Bois de Boulogne. He took pains to acquire some of the seeds for planting at his home at Louviers, only to find when he returned to the United States that the trees he had admired in Paris were *Aesculus glabra,* the Ohio buckeye!

It may have been Cousin Charles who introduced into the family the custom of bride and groom planting a pair of evergreen trees in proximity to one another at the time of their marriage (fig. 25). Possibly it was a practice he had observed among his Quaker neighbors. Three later generations of newlyweds to occupy Louviers, Eugene and Amy du Pont, Henry B. and Eleuthera Bradford du Pont, and William W. Laird, Jr. and his wife Winnifred, have perpetuated the custom, and their wedding trees flourish today on the grounds at Louviers.

After her marriage to a Philadelphia physician, Dr. Thomas MacKie Smith, Eleuthera, Irénée and Sophie's third daughter, made her home at Hagley, a short walk from Eleutherian Mills, then occupied by her younger brother Henry and his wife Louisa. Between the two homes was Nemours, built in 1824, where elder brother Alfred Victor and his wife Margaretta Lammot (Meta) and their children lived (see fig. 26). Hagley was the oldest dwelling in the du Pont domain, having been built in 1795 by Jacob Broom, from whom Irénée had purchased his first piece of Brandywine property in 1802.

Her diaries reveal Eleuthera as a dedicated gardener who habitually spent several hours a day either in the greenhouse that had been built to adjoin her living room or out in the garden if the weather was nice. These entries made during the spring and fall of 1840 give some idea of her gardening activities.

March 2: Gardening till near 11. Went over to sister's for Missouri bushes.

Fig. 25 Wedding trees on the grounds at Louviers. Photograph by Herzog.

March 3: Went to Barley Wood for shrubs. Brought up 35 and planted them all.

March 5: Picked first large bunch of violets.

March 18: Planted 56 plants.

September 30: To the exhibition with Meta and her daughters and Lina. The flowers very beautiful. Got a seed pod of a new kind.

Meta, Mrs. Alfred V. du Pont, was particularly fond of roses and had success growing many kinds in the garden at Nemours. Picking them was a temptation to the powdermen's children living nearby. Meta wrote, "The children of the place come in shoals to beg for a bunch, so I give rather than have them pulled to pieces."

In 1846 Eleuthera and her husband made an extended tour of the British Isles and the Continent, visiting abbeys, palaces, cathedrals, art galleries, battlefields, museums, literary shrines, hospitals, parks, and gardens. Keeping up the family practice—strongest among its female members—of writing long and frequent letters to close relatives, Eleuthera described and commented upon all that she and her husband saw, but her greatest enthusiasm was for flowers and plants of exceptional beauty or those that were new to her. About one of their trips in England she exclaimed to sister Victorine:

I never saw anything more lovely than our ride all the way to Chester. The Broom and Hawthorn in blossom on all the waysides & innumerable wild flowers different from ours. . . . Flags of various kinds, wall flowers and innumerable Stock gillies. At one place I saw the largest & finest white ones I ever beheld.

And she was quick to note that English railroad bridges, usually of stone or brick, had ivy growing over their sides and "always a flower pot at each side," a pleasing contrast to "our ugly railroad bridges."

At Eton Hall, seat of the Marquis of Westminster,

There were many shrubs and trees new to me; those I recognized were pink, white and red Hawthorn, now in bloom. Laburnums in profusion, Lilacks, Mountain ash also in bloom, white horse chestnuts & a quantity of some kind of laurel. . . .

We saw all the gardens, green houses, pineries, & hot houses, & I only wish you could have seen the flowers in the green houses, hundreds and hundreds I never saw before, most beautiful. The greatest variety of Fuschias too, many of the flowers an inch and a half long! The pansies

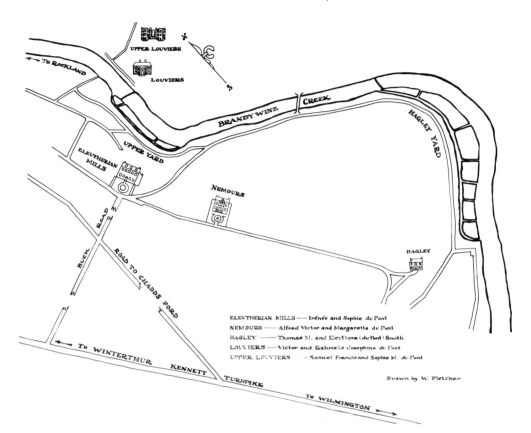

ELEUTHERIAN MILLS —— Irénée and Sophie du Pont
NEMOURS —— Alfred Victor and Margaretta du Pont
HAGLEY —— Thomas M. and Eleuthera (du Pont) Smith
LOUVIERS —— Victor and Gabrielle Josephine du Pont
UPPER LOUVIERS —— Samuel Francis and Sophie M. du Pont

Drawn by W. Fletcher

Fig. 26 Map showing the locations of the du Pont homes overlooking Brandywine Creek.

were most astounding, and I admired them so much that the man who went round with us culled me 7 or 8 of them, all of different colours. I have pressed 4 of them to give some idea of their size; I only wish they could keep their colours! He also gave me a branch of a new plant, the Rhodanthe Melligri, which keeps for ever like the Immortelles. It is however different in shape & of a beautiful pink. . . . The pineries were beautiful, some [pineapples] in bloom, some nearly ripe. We told the man about growing them in pure charcoal which seemed much to interest him.

A few weeks later the Smiths were in the botanical gardens at Edinburgh where, wrote Eleuthera, "I was for upward of two hours in a perfect wilderness of flowers & only wanted some of you to share my ecstasies." In the gardens at Chiswick she was delighted with "cape orchides" and "air plants" which "exceeded everything you could imagine." Eleuthera jotted down the names of certain plants she would like to have for her own garden and greenhouse at Hagley, for she planned to have an American nurseryman import them for her.

In France the Smiths stayed for a time with their nephew, James I. Bidermann, son of Mr. and Mrs. James A. Bidermann of Winterthur near Wilmington. Mrs. Bidermann was Evelina, the second daughter of Irénée and Sophie du Pont. Born in America in 1817, the younger Bidermann had gone to France to further his career as an engineer in railroad construction and had chosen to remain there. In their family garden at Brienon his wife Camille helped Eleuthera make a collection of seeds and gave her several flowers unknown to her to bring back to the United States. A relative of Camille's, Mrs. Gabriel Odier, added to the collection from her extensive garden and assisted Eleuthera in trying to find the seeds of "a kind of purple Centaurée, and a grey-black Scabious." Concluding her letter telling of these collecting activities, Eleuthera remarked, "I often wish I could, with a fairy's wand, send over some of those I have seen on this side of the ocean."

The Bidermanns took their visitors to see the old du Pont home, Bois-des-Fossés, near Chevannes, where they were warmly greeted by other relatives, the Bienaymé family, who now owned the property. Eleuthera's own words best describe this beloved spot from which her parents had departed most reluctantly forty-seven years earlier:

Mrs. Bienaymé & the young ladies escorted us round the garden and grounds. The house is much prettier & larger than I expected, & the barns, etc., are very numerous. We went thro the woods where she pointed out a number of oaks which stood there in Grand Pa's time. . . . Mrs. B. told me they had a wood at some distance all planted from trees or nuts sent from America by Grand Pa. They called it "l'Amérique," & I should much have liked to see it, but we had not time.

When we reached the meadow we separated—Tom returning to the house with Mrs. B. & I went with the girls to see a spot on the river where Grand Pa used to read & compose, & which bore, & *still bears* the name

89

of "Le cabinet de M. du Pont." It is a little grassy place under thick trees.

Without doubt the trees in "l'Amérique" were those which had matured from the seeds and cuttings that Irénée and Victor had taken there in 1801 for Philippe Harmand to plant; it will be remembered that, presciently, Victor had dubbed Bois-des-Fossés "Nursery of American Trees." The secluded woodland retreat beside the River Betz had been his father's outdoor study, where he meditated and wrote and where he may have revised his opus, *Philosophie de l'univers,* while in seclusion at Bois-des-Fossés in 1793 and 1794.

Eleuthera informed her sister Sophie, Mrs. Samuel Francis Du Pont of Upper Louviers, that she was bringing some flowers from the garden at Bois-des-Fossés to share with her and the other family gardeners. And Tom, her husband, had made an excellent sketch of the house which would give them some idea of its present appearance. One of Eleuthera's "Imports" was some *Myosotis*—forget-me-nots—which she propagated from a sprig grown at Bois-des-Fossés, which Cousin Léonie had given to her. She shared the flowers with Victorine, who planted them near the family dairy, whence they spread, blanketing a large area with a light blue covering of French forget-me-nots.

Her green thumb kept Eleuthera's greenhouse and garden overflowing. "I have been superintending and helping to arrange all my greenhouse," she later wrote to her cousin in France. "Every year the plants grow, and I get new ones besides, so that it is really a puzzle to find room for them all. Our parents were both very fond of flowers, and we inherited the taste." In January 1850 the Hagley barn caught fire, endangering the house; in her excitement the first thing Eleuthera thrust into a servant's hands to carry to safety was a pot of flowers.

Guests departing from Hagley went away laden with flowers and plants. With her sisters, Victorine at Eleutherian Mills, Sophie at Upper Louviers, and Evelina at Winterthur, and with her sisters-in-law, Meta at Nemours and Louisa, also at Eleutherian Mills, there was a steady exchange of things from one another's gardens and greenhouses. Seeds were shared and cuttings from new specimens passed around. A particularly beautiful flower or unusual shrub would be called to the attention of the entire family. Birthdays, anniversaries, the marriages of sons and daughters and of nephews and nieces, moves to a new home, the arrival of babies, and the frequent visits of relatives and close friends were all celebrated by gifts of flowers, flowering shrubs, and ornamentals and sometimes by the giving of young trees. The joy these family customs created shines through Mrs. Henry (Louisa) du Pont's note to her son, Henry Algernon, telling how the family celebrated her birthday on September 25, 1871: "I had lovely flowers brought me by every one so that our rooms were very pretty and quite filled with them. Even your father cut a bunch of roses and brought them in to me, making me feel quite young again."

Henry, her husband, who had been head of the family business for over twenty years, was too preoccupied directing the expanding powder factory and enlarging the family farms to give much attention to the gardens at Eleutherian Mills, so these became his wife's responsibility. With a large family of growing children demanding her time and attention, Louisa relied upon a gardener to do the work with a modicum of instruction from her. Growing in tubs at Eleutherian Mills were three flourishing lemon trees that Henry's father had planted some fifty years earlier, but that were fondly spoken of as "Mother's trees" by her daughters. Regularly for over half a century, with the approach of warm weather in April, they had been carried outdoors, and with the first chill of October air had been taken back into the house.

Her husband's tragic death in January 1852, by an accident for which she held herself responsible, almost killed Eleuthera. For a long time she remained inconsolable, a recluse in deep mourning. As time slowly assuaged her grief her spirits brightened, the transformation coming gradually as she tended the greenhouse plants and spent long hours amid the flowers in her garden. She wrote to her cousin Lilia in France telling her that

I am now enjoying the gardening and walking I have not been able to do before since the Spring of 1851. I wish I could make you see the beauty of my lilack hedge all around the garden, now in full bloom, and the pear trees in an orchard on one side and the apples on the other side, all a shower of blossoms and fragrance! I never enjoyed them as much!

Eleuthera survived her husband twenty-four years. Debilitated by cancer, her sole enjoyment during her last few years was her garden. The family greenhouses were searched for appropriate flowers for her funeral, but at midwinter they were very scarce.

Louisa wrote to Eleuthera's younger sister, Sophie, "I have only these few white flowers to send to my dear sister Eleuthera this morning. They are so few they seem scarcely worth sending over, except that I wanted to have some of the flowers of the *old greenhouse* she loved so much to be laid beside her."

Sophie and her husband, Captain Samuel Francis Du Pont, U.S.N., lived "over the crick" at Upper Louviers, a few hundred yards uphill from the banks of the Brandywine (plates 9, 10). For several years prior to their marriage in 1837, the house had been occupied by his mother, Mrs. Victor (Gabrielle) du Pont and his sister Amelia, but they had moved out to let the newlyweds have it as their home, which it remained until 1888. Here the love the married cousins shared for flowers and plants could be seen in the gardens which "Uncle Frank" and "Aunt Sophie" created around the house and which were tended for many years by John Lynch, their gardener.

During 1853 Captain and Mrs. Du Pont spent a large part of the year in New York City, where he was on loan from the Navy supervising the construction of the buildings for the Crystal Palace Exposition, the first world's fair held in the United States. Early in June he had to return to Wilmington, but because a recent accident prevented her from traveling, Sophie had to remain in their apartment in New York. The captain arrived at Upper Louviers just after a spring downpour, and the fresh rain-washed beauty of the place prompted him to take a leisurely walk around the house and through the gardens and woods. That evening, consistent in his practice of writing to Sophie almost every day he was away from her, Du Pont filled an eight-page letter, more than half of which was a paean in praise of Upper Louviers. In the sixteen years it had been their home it had never looked so beautiful! He regretted she could not be there with him to see it in its springtime loveliness, and he doubted if it would ever again wear this mantle of perfection, so he would try to capture it in words for her:

When I jumped out of the wagon at the kitchen door the first thing that struck me was that old Mrs. Lynch [the cook] was almost embowered with roses. On each side of the little gate those two roses have covered the whole fence, the one to the right literally covering the coal box and hiding it entirely from the yard. . . . I have only to tell you that the two small beds running from the back door, where every thing was dying out, were covered over with roses. The Agrippina, Louis Philippe, [and]

Plate 9 Upper Louviers. Photograph by Hampfler.

Plate 10 Entrance to Upper Louviers garden. Photograph by Hampfler.

red daily are large bushes covered with scarlet, making such a contrast with the Hermosa & pink daily as to surprise me almost as much as any thing I saw. Nothing can convey to you, however, the effect of the Gloria de Rosamond & Fellenberg touching each other—immediately opposite the Champney, covered as it never was before & then the dark red of the King of Holland. These bushes are fairly breaking down their supports. The one near the rain barrel is fast running round the kitchen piazza . . . its vigor is truly wonderful.

The Jean Duprez is also covered with its straw white and pink centres of blossoms. The jessamines are fast gaining the piazza top—and yet there is something handsomer than all these, as if it were saying, it is true my reign is a short one, but I can beat you all while it lasts—the Laure Devoust under your window, forming a bow of roses from the corner of the house to the piazza, the centre of the arch being immediately in the middle of the window, is handsomer than anything of the kind I ever saw in my life.

It is difficult to say what is the handsomest part of our grounds—for all that I have said of the show in the yard seems eclipsed by your bed in the upper part of the garden. Those running roses which we did not know what to do with are truly magnificent—one sheet five feet high of flowers & the foliage of one is very rare. The red one at the end near the dogwood that you think so much of is also covered, & the bushes have all trebled in size; the two Lewenbergs[?] are quadrupled & bent down with their loads of the largest roses I ever saw.

All in front of them is covered with verbenas of great brilliancy; with petunias, & John [the gardener] speaks in rapture of the beauty of a lily or iris which has just passed.

Now come round to the front. In the flower bed is not one solitary inch of the ground to be seen, neither is there a weed in it. From the edge of the grass border to the top of the June roses, also out, there presents itself an amphitheater or *gradin* closely packed of flowers of every hue, & of which no artistic gardener could improve the disposition. Near the house the roses again figure, the deep red with the light pink, & the Washington rose has covered the trunk of the locust tree, running up to the first branches. So also has the scarlet covered the small catalpa I started it on at the gate. In the center of the bed a white peony, of enormous circumference with the greatest quantity of flowers, forms a centre piece & shows off all the roses, flowers, poppies, etc., around it.

The African poppies are passing out it is true, leaving there however a very vivid imagination of their grandeur. John says they were splendid!!

The shrubbery has no notion of letting the flowers have all the glory & the weeping mock orange are in all their magnificence and grace. Eleu's is covered, & from the front piazza makes the most beautiful show. And to my surprise the laurels are doing well, the old one in the lawn quite covered and bright, making itself seen from all directions. The weeping mock oranges along the fence are also very handsome from the road.

John has the lawn perfect; the borders & the pretty sward under the dogwood, & the grass from the garden fence to the barn is also beautiful. . . . The walks are in perfect order & he has the whole place in perfect condition. The fruit is in keeping with everything else. Your cherry tree is covered, the limbs are fairly bent under the weight of the cherries. We shall have millions of raspberries & a great many pears. The pear trees that were moved have at last recovered & look beautifully healthy.

So much for our home, dearest Sophie; I thought you would like to be transported to it in thought & see all that I saw.

This is the most detailed description of a du Pont garden belonging to a second-generation member of the family, and for this reason it has been quoted at length. The Captain's words make the gardens at Upper Louviers bloom again in memory, the more remarkable because they were written by a man whose natural element had been the sea for over thirty-five years.

With less eloquence, but with admiration, a Wilmington newspaperman later made this comment about all the family gardens: "The residences of the Messrs. du Pont are pictures of beauty, surrounded as they are by magnificent lawns all aglow with flowers and shrubbery, among the primitive trees with which the banks of the Brandywine are fringed. It may truly be said at this time that up the Brandywine is magnificent, gorgeous, grand."

Mrs. Du Pont, "Aunt Sophie" to all the younger members of the family, was a semi-invalid confined much of the time to her upstairs sitting room and bedroom. But she was a gregarious and gallant soul, not given to self-pity or withdrawn from society. There was usually a house guest or two, some staying for weeks or months at a time. Regularly, almost daily, one of her sisters or sisters-in-law from the opposite shore visited her or sent a note if unable to get over the creek. Nephews and nieces who lived nearby, those married and home on a visit, and others on vacation from school or college seldom failed to call at Upper Louviers to pay their respects and spend some time with Aunt Sophie.

John Lynch, the gardener, became too old to care for the property and was retired. In his stead came Robert Trotter, a dour, bearded Scotsman who went daily to Mrs. Du Pont for instructions on the work to be done that day. If she thought her guests would enjoy it, and if she felt well enough, Aunt Sophie made a stately "progress" through the gardens seated in a specially designed, well-upholstered chair drawn by the gardener or his assistant, with Lydia, her personal maid, exercising watchful care.

The mistress of Upper Louviers knew all the flowers, plants, shrubs, and trees of her domain. She discussed them knowingly with her guests, pausing near certain ones for some detailed comment as her entourage moved leisurely along the garden walks. In the neatly tended beds bordered by low box hedges grew anemones, scented lemon verbenas, irises, geraniums, columbines, sweet peas, nasturtiums, primroses, and a galaxy of roses. Spotted about to give height, background, and contrasting colors were double pink altheas, lilacs, hawthorns, japonicas, and spireas. Growing wild in the woods nearby among the oak, beech, papaw, and tulip trees were vines and ground flowers—myrtle, blue hepatica, white windflower, May apple, and bloodroot. A tree cherished with special care was a fig tree that bore luscious purple figs which Aunt Sophie shared generously with the relatives across the creek. In late autumn this tree was "put to bed"— bent over, covered with straw, and a tin protecting cover placed on top of it.

In the greenhouse at Upper Louviers were plants of many kinds, some, one would assume, exotics brought home from distant places by her seafaring husband before his death in 1865. There were bright-hued amaranthus grown from cuttings sent over by sister-in-law Louisa from Eleutherian Mills. In turn, at different times Sophie gave Louisa some irises, roses, geraniums, and a night-blooming cereus. Louisa's note of thanks on one occasion read: "I am much pleased with the looks of my little package of seeds & thank you for all your trouble & for the sweet peas. I am very fond of them, having old associations of childhood connected with them. . . . I always had them in the garden so I feel almost a duty to keep them there."

Sophie's letters provide us with rare little gems of family garden history. Looking out of her upstairs sitting-room window on a hot August day in 1868, she was moved to include this remark in a letter to her nephew Dr. Alexis I. du Pont, who was away from home visiting relatives in Louisville, Kentucky:

I wish you could look out of my windows and see my beautiful Dhatura bushes with their profusion of long white bells! I know you would like them; they are very lovely to me, and an *unwritten* history of over 40 years comes back with their sweet odour, recalling the scenes and times and persons associated with their blooms. The first one was sent your Aunt Victorine from Alexandria in 1826, it having been sent from Madeira to Mrs. Cazenove in one of her husband's ships.

Mrs. Cazenove's husband was Anthony C. Cazenove, a merchant in Alexandria, Virginia, who was one of the early agents selling Du Pont powder. The two families had close ties of friendship, visiting back and forth, and the children attended the same schools.

In the fall, as the nights grew colder, the du Pont ladies would confer about moving the plants and flowers growing outdoors into their greenhouses. Their notes have survived; this is one of Louisa's to Sophie: "I am having flowers brought into the greenhouse today. Perhaps it is a little early but I thought it was safer." Sophie's more distant correspondents on matters horticultural included such professional growers and nurserymen as David Landreth of Bloomsdale Farm at Bristol, Pennsylvania, to whom in 1872 she sent some unusual apple grafts for identification. Landreth recognized the variety as one he had seen in an orchard near Burlington, New Jersey, and hazarded an opinion that it had been introduced into New Jersey by an exchange between Sophie's father, E. I. du Pont, and the statesman Elias Boudinot, who had his home near Burlington.

When Ellen, Louisa and Henry's daughter, married Alexander E. Irving in 1873 and began laying out a garden at her new home on Staten Island, Aunt Sophie had her gardener select bulbs, shrubs, roots, and cuttings, all of which were carefully packed in a barrel and sent to her niece. Ellen was delighted—"in raptures over all her plants"—her mother informed Sophie, for "no one here, surrounded by flowers, can imagine the pleasure they have given her. She tells me where she had planted everything and has had the greatest enjoyment." A similar "transplanting" of horticultural and floral items took place when Ellen's younger sister Sophie married Theophilus P. Chandler, a young architect, and set up housekeeping in the model community of Ridley Park, Pennsylvania.

CHAPTER VIII

Winterthur

The family love for flowers will be, I hope, continued in my children.
Mrs. Henry (Louisa) du Pont to
Mrs. Samuel F. (Sophie) du Pont, 1876

THERE was a crisis in the household of Louisa and Henry du
Pont at Eleutherian Mills in 1873 when the family gardener,
Charles Folgar, left their employ and departed in early March without informing them of his intentions. The furnace that heated the
greenhouse went out, the plants there remained untended, and the
plants and cut flowers in the home went unwatered. Mrs. du Pont
was angered by Folgar's thoughtlessness and quite concerned that
things might die from his neglect. Until a new man could be hired,
the garden chores were taken over by Patrick, one of the house
servants, who was assisted by Alex Burns, a powderman and a
knowledgeable amateur gardener.

The man who was hired was named James, last name not known,
formerly a gardener for Mrs. John Latimer, a Wilmington friend
of the du Ponts. James pleased his new mistress because "He wants to
do right and is anxious to hear what I want to have him do. I see
Mrs. Latimer's good training in him. He evidently has never been
allowed to cut down and uproot things without special permission,
which is a great comfort." Pleased though she was with James, it was
not long before Louisa found irksome the frequent consultations
with him that taxed her time and patience.

No doubt James was enlisted by Louisa and Henry in an undertaking that occupied them and their younger son, William, from April
to October in 1875. This was getting Winterthur, a property on the
Kennett Pike a few miles north of Greenville (fig. 27), ready to receive their eldest son, Henry Algernon, and his bride, Pauline Foster.
The newlyweds, who had married in late summer 1874, were on a
prolonged honeymoon and grand tour of Europe, and upon their

Fig. 27 Winterthur in 1884, the home of Henry A. and Pauline du Pont.

return they would be making their home at the 450-acre farm estate which Henry's father had acquired in 1867.

Winterthur had been a family property since 1839 when James A. Bidermann and his wife, Evelina Gabrielle du Pont, had moved there from their home, Hagley House, located near the powder mills. Bidermann had retired from the powder company after twenty-five years and had devoted his time to developing his new home as a gentleman's farm. At their home on Clenny Run, James and Evelina in time had a conservatory, a greenhouse, a forcing shed, a kitchen garden, a sunken garden, and beds of flowers for cutting.

Surrounding the home area were many kinds of evergreens, towering oak trees, beech, hickory, and tulip trees. A sloping hillside lawn close by the house was encircled with beautiful dogwoods. Until age and poor health forced them to give it up, the Bidermanns continued to be active gardeners, giving and receiving items from friends and other members of the family and exhibiting at farm fairs and garden shows. After their deaths Winterthur passed to their son, James I. Bidermann, who was making a career in French railroading and preferred to stay in France.

In 1867 he sold the property to his uncle, Henry du Pont, who made numerous improvements on the land and enlarged Winterthur by purchasing the neighboring Negendank farm and that of Peter Gregg, located between the Upper Yard of the powder mills and Winterthur. At that time tracks of the Wilmington and Reading Railroad were being laid across du Pont land, and a splendid old poplar tree approximately eighteen feet in circumference was on the right of way and would have to be cut down. Ruefully the elder du Pont noted to his son, "I fear we cannot save it as the R.R. comes too close to it. I will try, however, to get them to dodge it as such trees are getting rare in this part of the country." Losing a fine tree was akin to losing a long-time friend.

Despite a seemingly gruff exterior and total preoccupation with the family business and farms, the father was sensitive to the beauty of his Brandywine surroundings, though this was not often revealed, and not in a manner characteristic of his sisters. Commenting on the extreme lateness of spring, he observed to Henry Algernon on May 3, 1874:

This is the first Spring day we have had although there was ice this morning in the veranda gutters. But the leaves of the shrubbery are beginning to unfold; the forest trees are as black and leafless as winter. The willows have only begun to show life in the last two or three days. It is the most backward Spring I ever have seen. . . . The grass is beginning to get quite green and is beautiful. I suppose we must have Spring now.

Months before her son's marriage, Louisa had begun making frequent trips in her carriage up the Kennett Pike, accompanied sometimes by her husband and sometimes by William, to see what needed attention at Winterthur. On a bright fall day as she drove through the woods that led to the house, the splendor of the gold and scarlet foliage enthralled her. "I thought it would be difficult to find a lovelier home. . . . To my partial eyes it was beautiful." And before Henry and Pauline sailed on their European honeymoon in August 1874 they went to see their future home. After their visit Henry's mother sent a note across the creek to Aunt Sophie, telling her of the inspection trip. "We all went up to Winterthur today to see it and to show Pauline the spring and ferns and all the lovely wood paths around the house. She seems delighted with it & is a perfect sun-beam."

Henry's brother William, twenty years old, who later took up the life of a country squire, superintended the work being done in the woods, fields, meadows and gardens at Winterthur. Daily he rode from Eleutherian Mills up the Kennett Pike on horseback to direct the gardeners and the men clearing out the undergrowth, pruning trees, fencing, trimming shrubs, draining and grading the land, and he also helped to select the best location for new plantings. Though it was laborious, the younger du Pont enjoyed it and it was good for his none-too-robust health. Working with him was an experienced gardener named Bennett who had formerly been employed by Charles I. du Pont at Louviers. In a letter written to Henry A. and his bride, sojourning in France in May 1875, his mother exclaimed, "I wish you could see Winterthur in the first beauty of Spring! Every thing is now at last in leaf & the woods full of flowers. The gardeners seem industrious and attentive but the work there is most laborious, the whole ground is a mass of matted roots and briars."

At the end of that summer, in the midst of the September harvest and the vintage, Mrs. du Pont informed Henry and Pauline of the steps being taken to keep their larder filled and their house adorned with flowers for the approaching winter and the coming year:

You will have a supply of ordinary winter vegetables. The strawberry beds have just been planted . . . and the ground is ready for raspberries this fall as soon as the leaves drop from the plants. The asparagus bed is in good condition, planted last spring. Also some dwarf fruit trees & we have good grape vines well started ready for this fall. Willie would have had more fruit trees planted last Spring but we thought it better to wait & see what you thought of localities, etc. The old forcing house in the garden is to be put in order so that Pauline may have some flowers this winter.

And in a welcoming note to her new daughter-in-law shortly before the couple took up residence at Winterthur, Louisa exclaimed, "I am so glad, my dear Pauline, to think that you are coming to your country home before its autumn beauty has passed away. The woods are still full of flowers—fringed gentians, asters & golden rods—bright with their gold and crimson hues."

Colonel Henry A. du Pont, a dignified, ramrod-straight West Pointer and a veteran of the Civil War, was a lover of tradition and a conserver of the old. As the master of Winterthur for the next fifty years he made numerous changes to the gardens and grounds, but always with an eye to keeping what could be saved from the Bidermann days and from the plantings made by his parents and his brother (fig. 28). From his parents' garden and greenhouse, from Aunt Sophie, and from other kinfolk and friends came gifts of plants,

Fig. 28 Residence and part of garden at Winterthur, about 1900.

103

seeds, bulbs, flowers, and trees to add beauty and variety to Henry and Pauline's gardens and grounds. In acknowledging one gift from Aunt Sophie, Henry may have been implying that his wife was not blessed with the gardener's green thumb: "Pauline has planted the trailing arbutus, and I trust it may live." And, in time, there flowed from Winterthur returning tokens of floral loveliness to the Brandywine homes of relatives and friends: "The children yesterday [May 23, 1882] took a bouquet of lilies to Rokeby to Cousin Mary."

Like his father, Henry felt keenly the loss of trees that had stood regally tall and solid for centuries. When one fine specimen was struck by lightning, he sadly remarked, "I shall feel terribly if this injury should kill the poor old tree, one of the few remaining relics of the primeval forest." Lightning rods were soon mounted on the tops of the towering, broad-girth trees that thrust upward above all their neighbors, still seen today as one walks through the woods at Winterthur.

After his retirement from active management in the Du Pont Company in 1902, the Colonel gave much more time to enlarging and further developing the gardens, assisted by his son, Henry Francis du Pont. Young du Pont preferred gardener's tools to soldier's weapons. His father wished him to try for West Point to make a career in military service, but the counsel of a wise, observant relative, Mrs. Francis I. du Pont, persuaded him that his son by temperament and interest was not suited for a military career. Allowed to follow his own inclinations, Henry Francis chose to be gardener and agriculturist.

New greenhouses, potting sheds, and forcing houses were put up, a sunken garden and a water-lily pool were laid out, a new rose garden established, and a March Bank of early spring flowers planted. An early specialty of Winterthur were peonies, of which over two hundred different hybrids flourished in the Peony Garden. Father and son, the latter calling himself "Winterthur's head gardener," planted a Pinetum, a grove containing a great variety of conifers—fir, spruce, pine, hemlock, and cedar—which have since grown into splendid trees that perfume the air and delight the eye. Along the woodland paths among the oaks, beeches, hickory, and tulip trees, and in carefully selected open spaces, they planted white, red, pink, and mauve azaleas by the thousands—235 varieties in all—that paint the woods with great splotches and corridors of brilliant color from early April until July. Among them there later came two new varieties, one with dark blood-red flowers named 'Henry F. du Pont,' and a large-flowered blue-mauve "sport" called 'Winterthur.'

New types of flowering dogwood were placed among the older dogwoods and amid the native viburnums and spicebushes. Rhododendrons of several hues appeared in the woodland shades and in dappled patches of sunlight. The locations for other trees and shrubs —magnolias, paulownias, Judas trees, crab-apple trees, lilac bushes, forsythias, deutzias, and Scotch broom—were carefully selected to obtain the best effect of coloring and landscape vista. Some of these were planted around the perimeters of beautifully tended open stretches of lawn carpeting the earth between dense stands of trees.

As an arboretum and horticultural showplace, Winterthur is today one of the world's great gardens, open to the public and visited by thousands of people every year. The spring and fall months draw the greatest numbers, but it is a delightful place throughout all the year. Harold Bruce has captured the chronology of its changing beauty in his engagingly written book *The Gardens of Winterthur in All Seasons* (Viking, 1968), superbly illustrated by the photographs of Gottlieb and Hilda Hampfler. It is a tribute to the three generations that have perpetuated a family tradition that had its beginnings at Bois-des-Fossés in the French countryside during the 1770s and 1780s.

Henry Francis du Pont, who died in 1969, was well known in American and international horticultural circles, where he was regarded as both a connoisseur and a practical expert in gardening. As a director of E. I. du Pont de Nemours and Company since 1915, he continued to be listed among company stockholders as an "agriculturist." His extended travels to all parts of the world, visiting arboretums, nurseries, and other famous gardens and horticultural showplaces, resulted in the acquisition of many new and strange types of trees, flowers, and shrubs that now thrive and add their beauty to Winterthur (plates 11, 12).

Mr. du Pont served as officer, manager, adviser, or board member of numerous botanical and horticultural organizations at home and abroad. He was honored many times for his services and contributions to gardening. As recipient of the Elsie De Wolfe Award presented by the American Institute of Interior Designers in 1966 he was honored for the creation of the Winterthur Museum of Early American Decorative Arts and for a lifetime in which he gave talents and means to nurture incomparable outdoor loveliness in his gardens. The Garden Club of America conferred its Medal of Honor upon him with this citation:

He is conceded by fellow horticulturists to be one of the best, even the best gardener this country has ever produced. Since boyhood he has been interested in gardening. This culminated in the great achievement of his estate, Winterthur, where he established a botanical garden of dramatic beauty.

His grandmother Louisa's wish that "the family love for flowers will be, I hope, continued in my children" has been fulfilled beyond her fondest expectations.

CHAPTER IX

Longwood Gardens

No other single individual has done so much to foster a love of flowers in this country.

> Citation of Massachusetts Horticultural
> Society awarding its George Robert White
> Medal to Pierre S. du Pont, 1926

A FEW miles north and west of Winterthur, in the lower reaches of Chester County, Pennsylvania, is Longwood Gardens, another magnificent, world-famed showplace created by Pierre S. du Pont, cousin of the owner of Winterthur. A century before this section of pleasant rolling country became du Pont property, an arboretum covering thirty acres had been started here in 1800 by two brothers, Joshua and Samuel Peirce, who planted more than 250 different specimens of trees. Avenues of beech and maple trees were planted, and trees and shrubs not native to this part of Pennsylvania were brought in to establish Peirce's Park, which was later opened to the public (fig. 29). Showing a visitor through the park at mid-century, Joshua Peirce recalled that the soil had not proved suitable for farming, so he had planted it in peach trees but was plagued by neighborhood boys raiding the orchard. He and his brother then decided to plant something that could not be so readily pilfered and set about developing the arboretum.

But mingled with this practical decision there was botanical curiosity and, possibly, Quaker love for the things of nature. Other Peirces, notably another Joshua Peirce, a cousin who specialized in growing rare camellias at his Linnean Hill Nursery in the District of Columbia, were enthusiastic horticulturists. The Linnean Hill Nursery in Rock Creek valley occupied land where the Natural History Museum was built many years later. The visitor whom Joshua Peirce was showing around in 1850 was of the opinion that Peirce's Park was the finest artificial park in the country: "Here each tree is in itself perfect, and variety enhances the beauty of each."

The more unusual specimens planted by the Peirce brothers were a

Fig. 29 Peirce's Park, 1884.

yellow cucumber magnolia, a paulownia that grew to over fifteen feet in circumference, a Kentucky coffee-bean tree, bald cypresses from Maryland swamps or from Virginia's Dismal Swamp, a ginkgo from the Orient, and a rare English walnut grafted onto a black walnut. There were English and Irish yews, a clump of sugar maple trees, copper beeches, some splendid white pines, and French, Spanish, and American chestnut trees (fig. 30).

Near the old Peirce home that had been built in 1730 was a stand of spruce, hemlock, cedar, fir, holly, rhododendron, tree boxwood, and euonymus—some of which still flourish—that was called the "Evergreen Glade." On their visits to Philadelphia, the Peirces would make comparisons of the trees growing in the downtown squares of the Quaker City with the same kinds at Peirce's Park, and they estimated that theirs grew one to two feet more each year than those in the city. The Chester County botanist William Darlington,

Fig. 30 An avenue of trees in Longwood Gardens, 1910.

in his *Memorials of John Bartram and Humphry Marshall* (1849), said of the brothers, "Joshua and Samuel Peirce of East Marlborough began to adorn their premises by tasteful culture and planting; and they have produced an *arboretum* of evergreens and other elegant forest trees not surpassed in the United States." Two other writers on horticulture, Thomas Meehan, a Germantown nurseryman, in his *American Handbook of Ornamental Trees* (1853) and Josiah Hoopes in *The Book of Evergreens,* published in 1868, also called attention to the trees in Peirce's Park and made comparisons of some of them with specimens in Bartram's Gardens and on the Woodlands estate of William Hamilton.

It was the cutting down of some of the finest of these trees in 1906, and the likelihood of the destruction of more of them, that prompted Pierre S. du Pont (1870–1954), great-grandson of E. I. du Pont, to purchase the property. Just when the name "Longwood" had first been applied to it is not known. The farm of John Cox on the southern part of the original Penn grant of 1700 to George Peirce was known as Longwood, and a Quaker meetinghouse nearby has borne the name since the 1840s. It may have been derived from a long stretch of woodland extending from the nearby village of Hamorton southward to Sills' Mills.

Fifteen years were spent developing and enlarging the older arboretum (fig. 31) into what botanists acclaimed one of the horticultural wonders of America when Longwood Gardens was first opened to the public in 1921. What the Peirces had wrought was not undone by the new owner but given the best of care. His joy of discovery and the pleasure gained from working in the garden are evident in a letter written in May 1907, the first spring he occupied the new place:

This Spring has brought to light many plants whose presence we had not expected. The Spring flowers have been very fine and filled us with enthusiasm. I have lately taken great interest in the new garden that I have laid out in the small field immediately in front of the house. It is to be on the old-fashioned plan of straight walks and box borders at the edge of the flower beds. So far, considerable progress has been made, and I have set myself and guests to work planting flower seeds whenever I have opportunity.

Gardeners at Longwood were early instructed to maintain the park

Plate 11 Azalea woods at Winterthur. Photograph by Hampfler.

Plate 12 Daffodils along banks of Clenny Run, Winterthur. Photograph by Hampfler.

Plate 13 Fall display of chrysanthemums in the conservatory at Longwood Gardens.
Photograph by Hampfler.

Plate 14 Fountains in Longwood Gardens. Photograph by Hampfler.

in as near its original condition as possible. They were to cut and trim only as proper care demanded and they were to preserve its quaint characteristics of an older time. The blades of the lawn mowers were to be set high so they would not cut off the tops of the wild violets that carpeted the lawn encircling the house. No signs of neglect should be tolerated, but du Pont cautioned against over-neatness and excessive, fastidious care, a tendency he thought too prevalent on modern country places. Any tree damaged by wind or storm was to be treated only under the owner's direction. "The preservation and care of trees is considered of first importance, as their injury is irreparable" read his instruction in the Longwood employees' manual.

Mrs. du Pont shared her husband's enthusiasm for gardening and beautifying the landscape. This was demonstrated by her preference for a ten-mile "necklace of trees" given her on a certain anniversary occasion. In the early 1920s the Kennett Pike was being widened and improved, with the inevitable cutting down of trees that bordered it. Mrs. du Pont, later a director of the Garden Club of America, suggested to her husband that instead of the pearl necklace he contemplated giving her he should replace the lost trees by having new ones planted where the property owners along the road would consent to having them put in.

The happy consequence of this thoughtful act is enjoyed by every traveler on the Kennett Pike as he journeys on an expertly landscaped road free of commercial eyesores and advertising signs. To guarantee its wooded appearance in the future, in his deed of transfer giving the Kennett Turnpike to the states of Delaware and Pennsylvania in 1920, Pierre S. du Pont stipulated that the permission of every property owner on both sides of the road, throughout its entire length, had to be obtained before advertising signs could be erected at any point along its right of way. One arboreal landmark a short distance above Greenville, Delaware, was singled out for special care. The donor specified that "the State Highway Department shall protect and preserve by every practical means the ancient colonial pear tree at or near the entrance of the private road of Eugene E. du Pont." This was Dogwood, the property of a cousin. The tree, twisted, stunted, and 90 percent cement patches, in recent years put out a few leafing branches each spring until the summer of 1967

Fig. 31 The first garden at Longwood, adjacent to a corn field, 1909.

when it appeared dead. But from its root area there has since emerged a tall slender shoot, to all appearances a healthy offspring.

Fountains and flowing water fascinated the owner of Longwood all his life. When taken to the Centennial Exhibition of 1876 in Philadelphia as a boy of six he enjoyed most of all the fountains in Machinery Hall, where there were "jets of all kinds spurting like mad and without cease." He compared these with the fountain on the grounds at Nemours. "At home we had a garden fountain, with one jet, of the size of a knitting needle, turned on occasionally, closely watched, and turned off as soon as possible." This may explain why one of the early features at Longwood was an Italian water garden patterned after that of the Villa Gamberaia near Florence. Surrounded by linden trees, the water garden has four rectangular and two circular pools with bordering planted strips and a screen of tree boxwood and hemlocks at its northern end. Classic in balance and proportion and enhanced by decorative stonework, it becomes an enchanting scene as streams of shimmering water shoot heavenward and then arch downward into beautiful blue-tiled pools. In his travels at home and abroad, du Pont visited gardens searching for new flora and for design innovations he could adopt at Longwood.

Plants, shrubs, flowers, and trees of innumerable species, types, and variants, from the local and familiar to the rare exotics brought from abroad, grow in the outdoor gardens, on the grounds, in the greenhouses, and in the great bronze-and-glass conservatory, or orangery. The erection of the conservatory as a showplace for all to enjoy may have been the consequence of another boyhood experience. As a youngster of nine, Longwood's owner had stayed for a time with friends in Philadelphia, and on a walk with an "uncle," Frederic Graff, they passed the greenhouse of Matthias W. Baldwin, the locomotive manufacturer, located on Chestnut Street near Eleventh. The greenhouse was built with the long side paralleling Chestnut Street, making the full length of the interior easily visible to all passersby. Young Pierre learned from Mr. Graff that Baldwin had erected his greenhouse in this position because he loved flowers and plants and wanted them displayed so that others could also enjoy them; he resented that many fine privately owned collections were kept from public view. In notes for an autobiography that he was preparing to write in 1945, du Pont recalled that then and there he had resolved "that if ever I built a greenhouse it would be kept open to public view from within as well as from without. Time and destiny have enabled me to make good this self-made, if not selfish, promise."

The conservatory is the focal exhibit at Longwood (plate 13). Seasonal displays of unmatched loveliness appear at Eastertime: lilies, tulips, daffodils, hyacinths, cinerarias, ranunculuses, genistas and snapdragons. At Christmas the perfect grass quadrangle just inside the entrance glows with a border of thousands of poinsettias in flamboyant red, salmon pink, ivory, and white. Pacing the cycle of the seasons there are azaleas and acacias in the spring; roses, caladiums, cannas, and a medley of other summer flowers; chrysanthemums in the fall; and camellias and poinsettias in winter. In a desert garden grow many varieties of cacti and desert plants, and in a striking natural tropical setting are dozens of different palm trees.

Near the entrance to this tropical "house" are perpetually blooming orchids, from the commonplace to the extremely rare. The conservatory, about the size of a football field, covers over three acres and is technically equipped to produce almost any temperature and humidity environment desired for each of its many rooms and corridors, including a tropical mist room where pitcher plants thrive in the atmosphere of a rain forest. A writer impressed by all this in its setting of quiet, serene beauty was moved to exclaim, "To garden in the du Pont manner is big business."

Cultivation, classification, design, and arrangement are supervised by professional botanists, horticulturists, geneticists, and taxonomists, aided by experienced practical gardeners. Some staff members range far afield collecting new specimens, while others conduct hybridizing and other breeding experiments in the laboratories and greenhouses. Trips abroad to seek new specimens for cultivation in this country are usually conducted jointly with the U.S. Department of Agriculture, with which Longwood maintains a close relationship in explorations of this kind. Exchanges are made with parks, gardens, and other arboretums in this country and overseas, and all items from such sources are first observed and tested in the Experimental Greenhouse. The staff shares its knowledge and enthusiasm with the amateur gardeners of the region by conducting classes, lectures, and special demonstrations on many subjects. Guest lecturers and discussion sessions have become part of the Gardens' education program. In conjunction with the University of Delaware, Longwood is now offering a number of fellowships in ornamental horticulture by which students can earn a Master of Science degree in a two-year course of study. For their use and for staff members and qualified visitors, there is an excellent library with a wealth of books and periodical literature dealing with botany, horticulture, and related subjects.

There are other attractions at Longwood that liken it to the pleasure grounds that European royalty and nobility developed so lovingly and resplendently during the eighteenth and nineteenth centuries. The outdoor theater with its colored fountains and water screen which becomes a curtain; the plays, concerts, and musical dramas presented on its stage; the formal box gardens beneath the esplanade of the conservatory, with their immense fountains on which symphonies of changing colored lights are spectacularly played (plate 14); the waterfall and chimes tower; the grand ballroom of the conservatory reverberating to the music from the great organ, one of the most complex and versatile ever built—these evoke Versailles, Blenheim, and Hampton Court, the Xanadus of another age, where crowned heads and aristocracy gathered to revel in beauty and to find relaxation but which the commoner entered only as artisan or performer.

At Longwood these features were introduced as desirable appurtenances to Pierre S. du Pont's single purpose: to make the Gardens a "horticultural display for the benefit and enjoyment of the public." Such is the simple, direct statement in his will that created the Longwood Foundation to maintain the Gardens in perpetuity after his death. His participation in horticultural matters had begun early in life and remained his major avocation, second only to his business career, an atavistic, expanded echo of his great-grandfather, E. I. du Pont. The continuance of his garden is assured, as witness the statement of his nephew, Henry B. du Pont, president of the Longwood Foundation before his death in 1970: "The horticultural displays and thousands of trees which form a part of Longwood Gardens have been left to us along with funds for their perpetuation. We wish to encourage and welcome all who enjoy nature to share the aesthetic benefits which its beauty bestows."

Garden clubs, horticultural societies, and forestry associations bestowed honors and awards upon the founder of Longwood for the "ever green" memorial he erected to a cherished family tradition. Here the casual visitor who loves beauty, the flower enthusiast, the entranced child, the amateur gardener with serious purpose, the wanderer along woodland walks, and the professional botanist are the public that derives enjoyment and instruction from the du Pont desire to grow things, a way of life that had its beginnings at Bois-des-Fossés nearly two centuries ago.

CHAPTER X

The New and Old Gardens at Eleutherian Mills

How deeply seated in the human heart is the liking for gardens and gardening.

Alexander Smith

DU PONT family occupancy of Eleutherian Mills came to a sudden end early in October 1890, when a thunderous, devastating explosion destroyed the mills in the Upper Yard and killed twelve workmen. Thirty homes located close to the mills were totally wrecked and the du Pont residence made uninhabitable, with cracked walls, heaved-up floors, and every door and window shattered.

A local reporter viewing the scene soon after the disaster pictured the desolation: "This was once covered with the habitations of men, with fertile gardens of tomatoes, pumpkins, and other fruits and vegetables. Now this tract is a desolate place devoid alike of houses and plants." Mrs. Henry du Pont, a widow since the death of her husband the preceding August, and to whom this had been home since her marriage in 1837, wrote with saddened heart to a relative, "Our dear old home is a perfect wreck—literally broken to pieces. We have, of course, been obliged to leave it and have moved to a house belonging to my son Willie, but our hearts still cling to the old place." After nearly ninety years of occupancy by four generations of the family, the home and garden had to be abandoned.

Under the direction of Eugene du Pont, a nephew who had succeeded Henry du Pont as head of the firm, the powder mills were speedily rebuilt and put into operation, workmen's homes rebuilt and repaired, and the du Pont residence boarded up. What remained of the old garden that E. I. du Pont had created and which his sons and daughters had cared for over the years was cleared off and turned into grazing land as part of the Du Pont Company's farming operations. In 1892 the dwelling was made structurally sound and converted into quarters for the Brandywine Club, a powdermen's social and recreational center with pool tables, card room, library, lunch room, bowling lanes, and shower rooms. This was its role until the outbreak of World War I, when a contingent of soldiers encamped on the site of the old garden as a protective force against possible sabotage of the powder mills, and their officers were billeted in the residence. For a few years after the war the house was occupied by the head farmer and his family and the garden site became a potato field and vegetable patch. When the mills were closed down in 1921–1922, Colonel Henry A. du Pont purchased the mill and residential properties that constituted Eleutherian Mills from the Du Pont Company and gave it to his daughter, Mrs. Francis B. (Louise) Crowninshield and her husband. The gift of the old home property

Fig. 32 The twentieth-century classical gardens at Eleutherian Mills. Photograph by Lautman.

carried with it a promise to her father that they would maintain it and occupy it for a part of each year. Mrs. Crowninshield had been born at Winterthur in 1877 and had grown up there, but as a child she had enjoyed many happy times staying with her grandparents at Eleutherian Mills. Now it was hers.

The new owners took possession in 1923 and began renovating and furnishing the home in Federal period style apropos of when her great-grandparents had occupied it (plate 15). They knew of the old garden at the front of the house, for Mrs. Crowninshield had been in it many times as a child, but they turned it into lawn, with some cutting beds of flowers, and focused their attention upon the abandoned mills at the back of the residence extending down the slope to Brandywine Creek. Here they set for themselves the ambitious project of transforming this unsightly industrial area into an intriguing and fascinating arrangement of terraced gardens.

Acting as their own designers and landscape architects, the Crowninshields tore down most of the mill structures and on the foundation walls created a Mediterranean-style classical garden that could be a perfect setting for the contemplative stroll of a Greek philosopher or the entertainment of a Roman senator. It was the work of a number of years and, as it took shape, flagstone walks bordered by low-growing box became paths between avenues of tall, tapered conifers beneath which ground flowers cluster and annuals bloom in bright and varied hues. One walk leads to a sunken pool, at the end of which is a temple ruin with a mosaic Pegasus in its tiled floor (fig. 32). A vista of Doric columns and towering evergreens, amid which stand statues from the pantheon of Greek and Roman heroes and mythological deities, is seen from the temple plaza. In grottoes and shadowed niches of vine-covered ruins, Pan plays his pipe accompanied by the musical tinkling of a flowing spring, and nearby Aphrodite poses in eternal pagan loveliness.

The Crowninshield gardens are an ingenious blending of the formal and the natural, of restored antiquity imposed upon preserved vestiges of the more recent past. Brick-arched tunnels lead to the subterranean furnace remains of the old refinery, on top of which beds of flowers blossom in brilliant colors. Huge saltpeter kettles surmount brick columns marking the bounds of the old building, dark metallic counterpoints to the sculptured marble figures of Mercury, Jason, and Minerva standing on their pedestals nearby,

Plate 15 Eleutherian Mills. Photograph by Lautman.

Plate 16 Raceway in Hagley Yard. Photograph by Hampfler.

and a raceway of murmuring water that once brought power to turn the wheels of the mills courses the length of the garden, its stone walls festooned with gnarled wisteria and other clinging vines. The eye encompasses the century-old dam across the stream as part of the garden view, and the water flowering over it forms the eastern boundary of the garden.

When described in words, such juxtapositions are jarring because of their seeming incongruity. In actuality, amid the evergreens, boxwoods, forsythias, azaleas, dogwoods, flowering cherry trees and other ornamental plantings, the eye delights in the medley of colors and the beautiful panoramas that bear evidence of the tastes and originality of the garden's creators. As one visitor observed, it is a scene reminiscent of a Hubert Robert landscape. Here is an overlay of two du Pont traditions, the horticultural and the industrial, blended into a truly unusual garden that is most beautiful in the spring of the year.

Guests of the Crowninshields were immediately made aware of the continuance of another family custom upon crossing the threshold of Eleutherian Mills—the profusion of potted plants and flowers the entire length of the central hallway, and the many arrangements of cut flowers that lent fragrance and color to every part of the house and gave the impression that the garden had been brought indoors. A century earlier Mrs. Crowninshield's great-aunt Victorine had written, "The diningroom is almost like a greenhouse." Some of these flowers came from the new garden, others from the greenhouse erected on the north side of the barn and from the cutting beds on the site of the old garden.

The gardening interests of the Crowninshields extended far beyond their home garden on the Brandywine and the garden at their residence on Peach's Point at Marblehead in Massachusetts. Mrs. Crowninshield was an active member of a number of garden clubs and horticultural societies. She advised and assisted in the restoration of several gardens connected with historic houses, and she was a director of the Association for the Arnold Arboretum. A regular exhibitor at flower shows and horticultural exhibits, Mrs. Crowninshield received a number of prizes, one being the Albert C. Burrage Gold Vase of the Massachusetts Horticultural Society for the most outstanding exhibit of the year in 1937. As a vice-president of the Garden Club of America she participated in the roadside

Fig. 33 A view of the terraced gardens at the Crowninshield home. Photograph by Hampfler.

Fig. 34 An avenue of tapered conifers in the Crowninshield gardens. Photograph by Hampfler.

beautification projects of that organization, and in 1950 she received its Achievement Award, an honor she prized highly. Following her death in 1958, friends and relatives decorated and furnished a meeting room in her memory in the New York City headquarters of the Garden Club of America and named it the "Louise du Pont Crowninshield Room."

A few years before her death Mrs. Crowninshield gave Eleutherian Mills, including the residence, gardens, and surrounding acreage, to the Eleutherian Mills-Hagley Foundation, Incorporated. This foundation maintains the Hagley Museum a mile downstream at the lower end of the Hagley Yard, another creekside area of Du Pont Company mills where black powder had been manufactured until 1922. Visitors to the museum, which contains exhibits depicting the beginnings and the growth of American industry, are invited to walk or to ride a jitney through the Hagley Yard and, in scheduled periods during the spring and fall of each year, to continue the ride upstream to Eleutherian Mills. Though many of the small graystone mills remain, empty shells at the edge of the stream, the Hagley Yard shows none of the ugliness and shabby neglect of an abandoned industrial site. Soon after the mills ceased operating in the 1920s, another great-granddaughter of E. I. du Pont, Mrs. Charles (Louisa du Pont) Copeland, and her son Lammot du Pont Copeland began transforming the yard into a beautifully landscaped parkland and woodland preserve (plate 16).

Larger, older hardwood trees that had been planted decades ago and that had long served as buffers to hurtling debris in explosions—oaks, hickories, maples, cypresses, walnuts, and sycamores—were well cared for. Ornamental trees such as blue Atlas cedars and paulownias were planted in carefully chosen spots, the banks of the raceway lined with ginkgo trees, and hollies of many types were dotted about the grounds. Along the powder-yard road, flowering cherry trees and dogwoods, white, red, and pink, were put in, some of the dogwoods showing evidence of grafts by the pink and white blossoms found on the same tree. Massive clusters of deep red azaleas contrast brightly against the dark green of evergreens, and a stand of flame azalea growing on the site of a gunpowder press house glows in brilliant orange. Bare spots were covered with myrtle, periwinkle, pachysandra, and other ground covers, and clumps of early spring flowers—squills, blue hepaticas, narcissuses, jonquils, and daffodils—

everywhere grace the slopes and banks of the old powder yard. Back into this protected area have come many small woodland creatures, and occasionally a deer is seen by the keen-eyed visitor. But most visible are the scores of Canada geese that have made it a round-the-year home, for it is a wildlife sanctuary where geese and ducks and numerous other birds may nest and raise their young undisturbed by humans. Abundantly apparent are vestiges of the yard's industrial past which tell something of its history, but the visitor passing through it on his way to Eleutherian Mills becomes aware that nature, with some assistance from man, has been reclaiming this lovely wooded glen.

In its program of preservation and restoration aimed at picturing the industrial and the agricultural and domestic activities and patterns of living of this community during the nineteenth century, the museum has opened to the public the du Pont residence at Eleutherian Mills, with its attractive Federal period furnishings, the first office which served as company headquarters from 1837 to 1891, the private workshop of Lammot du Pont, a grandson of the company's founder, and a large stone barn containing exhibits of agricultural tools and farm and family vehicles.

Most recently the museum has begun the task of restoring the old garden begun by E. I. du Pont in 1802 but which had been lost sight of since the 1890s. Its site, two acres in extent, at the front or west side of the residence and only a few steps from the barn, has been carefully excavated by archaeologists each summer since 1968. Using scientific detection devices and guided by sketches and manuscript references that have survived, its buried physical features have been uncovered to a degree that will assure authentic reconstruction (fig. 35). The outer bounds of the garden have been fixed; the yellow gravel paths, some with stone drains beneath, have been established; the well has been uncapped; the foundations of the cold frame laid open; the post holes of the summer house or gazebo that stood near the rose garden have been found; and the foundation walls of the greenhouse, with brick flue and furnace room remains, have been excavated several feet beneath ground level. The findings of the archaeologists confirm in almost every detail the location of these structures as they appear on the sketch (page 72) drawn by Mrs. Victorine du Pont Foster, remembering the garden as it appeared about 1880. Restoration now under way is guided by these sources,

Fig. 35 Archaeological excavation at Eleutherian Mills on the site of the du Pont garden now under restoration. Photograph by Herzog.

and the flowers, plants, herbs, fruits, shrubs, and trees now being planted are those that were familiar to Irénée and Sophie du Pont and to their children and grandchildren for the nearly ninety years this was their family garden. Recapturing the beauty and atmosphere of this "old-fashioned" garden with the patterns, colors, and scents of its abundant and richly varied plant materials will be prolonged over a span of time, for bringing a garden into bloom must be done at nature's pace.

When he first arrived in the United States in the year 1800, Irénée du Pont foresaw his future in this country as a "Botaniste." Instead, circumstances led him to establish a business that has gained recognition as the leading enterprise of its kind throughout the world. It is clear, however, that neither he nor his descendants ever forsook the soil. Symbolically, with one foot in the powder yard and the other in his garden and farm, du Pont combined vocation and avocation with gratifying results. Among these was the imbuing of his children with a love of nature, a desire to better understand its seeming mysteries, and an appreciation of its utility and beauty. Thus began a recurrent pattern of living that clings to the rural setting, a home with gardens set close by fields and woodland. It is a tradition that continues into the present and one which helps make northern Delaware and nearby Pennsylvania a region of horticultural distinction.

Eleutherian Mills: Garden and Orchard List

A list of flowers, plants, shrubs, vines, fruits, berries, herbs, vegetables, trees and fruit trees in the garden and orchard of Eleuthère Irénée du Pont, 1802-1834.

Flowers

Asphodel	*Albuca*
Aster	*Aster novae-angliae*
Black-eyed Susan	*Thunbergia alata*
Buttercup	*Ranunculus repens* and *R. pleniforus*
Canterbury Bell	*Campanula medium*
Cardinal Flower	*Lobelia cardinalis*
Chrysanthemum	*Chrysanthemum morifolium*
Columbine	*Aquilegia*
Coreopsis	*Coreopsis grandiflora*
Crocus	*Crocus*
Daffodil (white)	*Narcissus*
Dahlia	*Dahlia pinnata*
Daisy (Pyrethrum or Painted)	*Chrysanthemum coccineum*
Dianthus	*Silene caroliniana*
Evening Primrose	*Oenothera odorata*
French Honeysuckle	*Hedysarum coronarium*
Gilliflower, or Common Stock	*Matthiola incana*
Hyacinth	*Hyacinthus orientalis*
Iris, or Blue Flag	*Iris versicolor*
Jonquil	*Narcissus jonquilla*
Larkspur	*Delphinium ajacis*
Lily of the Valley	*Convallaria majalis*
Live Forever	*Sempervivum*
London Pride	*Saxifraga umbrosa*
Madagascar Periwinkle	*Vinca rosea*
May Rose	*Viburnum opulus*
Mignonette	*Reseda odorata*

Nasturtium	*Tropaeolum majus*
Pansy	*Viola tricolor*
Periwinkle	*Vinca minor*
Phlox (Creeping)	*Phlox subulata*
Polyanthus	*Primula X polyantha*
Poppy	*Papaver orientale*
Purple Eternal Flower	*Xeranthemum*
Rattlebox	*Crotalaria*
Roses	*Rosa*
Beau Cramoisi Royal	Monsieur Rouge
Bengale de toute l'année	Napoleon
Champney's Pink Cluster	Perpetuelle
Couleur de Bronze	Pourpre foncé
Cuisse de Nymphe	Rose à cent feuilles
Grand Monarque	Rose des quatre saisons
Impératrice Josephine	Rose du Roi
Jaune Double	Rose pompone
Marie Louise	Rose ponceau
Monsieur Blanc	Sultane favorite
Scarlet Sage	*Salvia splendens*
Spurge	*Euphorbia*
Sunflower	*Helianthus annuus*
Sweet Pea	*Lathyrus odoratus*
Tobacco Plant	*Nicotiana tabacum*
Tuberose	*Polianthes tuberosa*
Tulip (dwarf)	*Tulipa*
Violet	*Viola*
Wallflower	*Cheiranthus cheiri*
Yellow Primrose	*Primula auricula*

Plants, Shrubs, and Vines

Angel's Trumpet	*Datura suaveolens*
Butterfly Pea	*Clitoria ternatea*
Coronilla	*Coronilla glauca*
Dwarf Morning Glory	*Convolvulus tricolor*
Fumitory	*Fumaria officinalis*
Fuschia	*Fuschia coccinea*
Golden Chain Tree	*Laburnum anagyroides*
Hollyhock	*Althea rosea*
Honeysuckle	*Lonicera*

Japanese Camellia	*Camellia japonica*
Jessamine	*Jasminum*
Jupiter's Beard	*Anthyllis barba-jovis*
Lilac	*Syringa vulgaris*
Meadowsweet	*Spiraea alba*
Missouri Currant	*Ribes odorata*
Moonseed	*Menispermum canadense*
Morning Glory	*Ipomaea purpurea*
Mountain Laurel	*Kalmia latifolia*
Peruvian Justicia	*Justicia peruviana*
Rose of Sharon	*Hibiscus syriacus*
Scotch Broom	*Cytisus scopularius*
Silver Bell	*Halesia carolina*
Snowberry	*Symphoricarpus albus*
Steeplebush	*Spiraea tomentosa*

Herbs

Sweet Basil	*Osimum basilicum*
Caraway	*Carum carvi*
Cochlearia (Scurvy Grass)	*Cochlearis officinalis*
Sweet Fennel	*Foeniculum vulgare*
Garlic	*Allium sativum*
Lavender	*Lavandula spica*
Sweet Marjoram	*Majorana hortensis*
Salsify (Oyster Plant)	*Tragopogon porrifolius*
Summer Savory	*Satureia hortensis*
Tarragon	*Artemisia dracunculus*

Vegetables

Artichoke	*Cynara scolymus*
Bonavista Bean	*Phaseolus* sp.
Long Red Beet	*Beta vulgaris*
Purple Cape Broccoli	*Brassica oleracea* var. *italica*
Cauliflower Broccoli	
Early York Cabbage	*Brassica oleracea* var. *capitata*
Long Orange Carrot	*Daucus carota* var. *sativa*
Early Horn Carrot	
Cauliflower	*Brassica oleracea* var. *botrytis*

Cucumber	*Cucumis sativus*
Green Curled Endive	*Cichorium endivia*
Broad Batavian Endive	
Lettuce	*Lactuca sativa*
Onion	*Allium cepa*
Large Parsnip	*Pastinaca sativa*
Bishop's Early Dwarf Pea	*Pisum sativum*
Glory of England Pea	
Radish	*Raphanus sativus*
Early Round Spinach	*Spinacia oleracea*
Late Prickly Spinach.	
Early Turnip	*Brassica rapa*

Fruits and Berries

Buffalo Berry	*Shepherdia argentea*
Cantaloupe	*Cucumis melo* var. *cantalupensis*
Currant	*Ribes sativa*
Gooseberry	*Ribes grossularia*
Grapes	*Vitis vinifera*
Chasselas	
Muscat blanc	
Muscat violet	
Précox	
Melon	*Cucumis melo*
Raspberry	*Rubus idaeus*
Rhubarb	*Rheum rhaponticum*
Strawberry	*Fragaria chiloensis* var. *ananassa*
Apple Seeded Watermelon	*Citrullus vulgaris*

Trees

American Chestnut	*Castanea dentata*
Bottlebrush Buckeye	*Aesculus parviflora*
Buckeye	*Aesculus*
Franklinia	*Franklinia alatamaha*
French Chestnut	*Castanea sativa*
Hazel Nut	*Corylus colurna*
Honey Locust	*Gleditsia triacanthos*

Japanese Pagoda Tree, or	
Chinese Scholar Tree	*Sophora japonica*
Lemon Tree	*Citrus limon*
Linden	*Tilia europaea*
Mimosa or Silk Tree	*Albizia julibrissin*
Mulberry	*Morus alba*
Orange Tree	*Citrus sinensis*
Pecan	*Carya illinoensis*
Persimmon	*Diospyros virginiana*
Smoke Tree	*Cotinus coggygria*
White Oak	*Quercus alba*

Pears

Angélique de Bordeaux	Epine d'été
Angleterre	Epine d'hiver
Aurate	Fondante de Brest
Bergamote d'automne	Fondante d'été
Bergamote de Pâques	Franchi Panne
Bergamote Suisse Panaché	Gilogile
Beurré	Martin-sec
Bezy d'Echassery	Messire-Jean
Bezy de Chaumontel	Muscat Robert
Bezy de la Motte	Orange musquée
Bezy de Montigny	Poire sans peau
Bon-Chrétien d'Auch	Rousselet de Rheims
Bon-Chrétien d'été	Royale d'hiver
Bon-Chrétien d'hiver	Saint-Germain
Catillac	Seckle Pear
Colmar	Sucre vert
Crassane	Sylvange
Cuisse-Madame	Tonneau deuxième variété
Doyenné blanc	Tonneau première variété
Doyenné doré	Virgouleuse
Epargne	

Apples

Anis	Azeroly
Api	Bough Apple

137

Calville blanc d'hiver
Calville rouge d'hiver
Court-pendu
Early Redstreak
Fall Pippin
Green Pippin
King Apple
Late Redstreak
McMahon's Superior
Monstrous Pippin
Newark Pippin
Newtown Pippin

Pigeonnet
Rambour d'été
Reinette du Canada
Reinette franche
Reinette grise
Seek-No-Further
Spitzemberg
Summer Pippin
Uncle Jacob's Sweet
Winter Pearmain
Winter Pippin

Peaches

Admirable
A Feuilles de Fougère
A Fleurs Blanches
Algerine Winter
Belle Chevreuse
Belle et Bonne
Belle Pêche
Bergen Point
Blood
Brevoort's Noblesse
Brevoort's Pineapple Clingstone
Butler's Fine Early
Columbia
Double Blossom
Double Fair
Double Montagne
Double Swalsh
Early Large Newington
Early Redcheek
Elizabeth Peach
English Chancellor
Grosse Mignonne
Heath
Kennedy's Carolina Lemon Clingstone

Large Malacatune
Large White
Lemon
Melting Peach
Morris's Red Rareripe
Morris's White Luscious
New York Rareripe
Non Pareille
Oldmixon Clingstone
Pêche à larges feuilles
Pêche blanche
Pêche des français
Pêche excellente
Pêche rouge
Pineapple
Polichinelle Peach
Téton de Venus
Très Belle Pêche
Vermeille
Very Red Peach
White Incomparable
White Nutmeg
Williamson's New York

Cherries

Anglaise
Anglaise hâtive
Bigarreau à gros fruit
Black Heart
Blanche à gros fruit
Cerise de la Toussaint
Griotte d'Allemagne

Griotte de Hollande
Gros Gobet
Guigne Peintresse
Mammoth
Montmorency
Royal May Duke

Plums

Gros Monsieur
Mirabelle
Monsieur hâtif
Perdrigon violet

Reine-Claude
Reine-Claude violette
Sainte-Catherine

Other Fruit and Nut Trees

Black Mulberry
Filbert
Japan Pear

Medlar
Peach Apricot
Persimmon

E. I. du Pont, Botaniste

was composed and printed by
Connecticut Printers, Inc., Hartford, Connecticut,
and bound by Complete Books Company,
Philadelphia, Pennsylvania.
The text paper is Mohawk Superfine, and the
paper for the color illustrations is
Warren's Cameo Brilliant.
The types are Granjon and Garamond.
Design is by Edward G. Foss.